TAROT FOR GRIEF

Steve Hounsome

TAROT FOR GRIEF

© 2022 Steve Hounsome

ISBN 9781899878581

ALL RIGHTS RESERVED

For Laura

"Grief is the price we pay for Love"

Queen Elizabeth II - 21/04/1926 - 08/09/2022

ACKNOWLEDGEMENTS

Cover Picture photo by David Mceachan from the website www.pexels.com

Tarot Card on the front cover from The Tarot Therapy Deck by Steve Hounsome

All the references to card images and illustrations in this book are to the Rider Waite Smith deck, since this is the most widely known one in use and so many other decks are derivatives of this. You are of course, free to use the deck of your choice and I recommend responding to the cards appearing for you in the same manner that you will see outlined in Chapter 5 'My Grief Process'.

50% of the proceeds from sales of this book will be donated to the charity MIND. This is a charity with the motto 'for better mental health'. I have chosen this charity because Laura faced some mental health issues during her life and we know this was close to her heart. Please see the Resources page at the end of the book for their website and other relevant charities.

CONTENTS

INTRODUCTION

'Grief is a process of Healing'

*'What is left ungrieved remains stored
in the body, heart, (mind) and soul'*

Elizabeth Kübler-Ross 'On Grief and Grieving'

To understand the intention of writing this book and the method of its creation, it is necessary to share the process that led to it.

This began at the end of October 2020 when my wife Amy was diagnosed with Stage 4 lung cancer. We were told this was 'treatable, not curable'. She was not classed as being terminal but we were clearly told, and reminded at intervals, that her treatment was to prolong her life and maintain its quality, rather than any attempt at a cure. There followed four months of chemotherapy, followed by radiotherapy, then ongoing immunotherapy every three weeks, which continued for some eighteen months.

Quite apart from the disease and diagnosis itself, the cost of all this has been great in all kinds of different ways. Amy had to sacrifice her hair, a big thing for most women perhaps but, massive for her as it was waist length. Our regular meetings and workshops teaching Tarot and related subjects (how we made our living), held at home for many years and at the time successfully shifted to online events due to the Covid 19 pandemic, had to stop so we could focus fully on Amy's treatment and care. The spread of Covid also meant full isolation for us, since Amy's immune system had effectively been destroyed by the chemo. As I write, restrictions are lifted but we have to maintain caution when we go anywhere. There have been many other costs as well.

Having worked with the Tarot for 40 years, one of the things that occupied my mind during this time was how the Tarot could be used to help cancer sufferers. If you are familiar with my work you will know that I advocate the use of Tarot in therapeutic and developmental ways, but beyond this generalization, I really could not see what other ways it could be utilised, or in a way specifically relating to those living with cancer.

It should perhaps be said here that there is a school of thought which suggests that the appearance of cancer can be related in some instances to unexpressed grief, and arguably especially so with lung cancer. Whilst research that has been done in this area has offered no conclusive proof of a link, it has to be said that this research takes a scientific approach, but we are largely not in the realm of science in this perspective.

During the time following Amy's diagnosis and ongoing treatment, I focused my work on teaching Tarot courses by distance-learning, students sending in written and recorded work and this, together with Amy's care, kept me occupied and I am glad to say, both flourished. This situation remains at the time of writing.

Then, on 27th January 2022, our eldest daughter Laura tragically died suddenly. Four days before she choked on some coffee, and the coughing caused a tear in her lungs, which collapsed. This was exacerbated by her lifelong asthma. She went into cardiac arrest. Ambulance crews revived her but her brain had been starved of oxygen for eighteen minutes. She was kept on life support for four days but following all necessary procedures and checks, she was pronounced dead.

Laura was actually my step-daughter but our relationship had become one of Daddy and Daughter, as it has with her younger sister Kate, I am proud to say. Any step-parent reading this will know this sense, and therefore the accompanying loss. Laura was just 32 and was eighteen months into a degree to become qualified as a Radiologist, something she had been aiming for in her nursing career since she began it, aged 18. She has two boys, aged 6 and 7 at the time of her death, and a husband. Her loss is simply massive, as anyone who has lost a child, partner, or sibling will know.

As part of my grief process I turned to the Tarot, initially just taking a card to see what I would get, in some hope of having something to at least cling to. As I sat with this process – details of which will be explained in this book – I began to see how I could both use the Tarot to help myself in my own grief, as well as find an answer to my earlier impulse and desire to show how the Tarot could help those suffering with cancer, or any such scenario.

Whilst not directly focused on the subject of cancer, I hope this book will help some people who have lost someone to this disease, of which there are of course, way too many - one in two of us now will have some form of cancer in our lives. I began to consider the idea of writing a book about how the Tarot can be used to help with our grief process and further research proved that it was eminently suited, as I hope you will see. In saying this I am very mindful of 'preparatory grief' as it is known – the process of grieving before the loss of someone, which we have come to know. I consider this to be a huge aspect of grief and one that requires great recognition and discussion. I hope this book will be put to use by those engaged with this process.

As I write this book, I am 57 years old. Of course the general principle is that the longer you live, the more likely you are to experience the death of loved ones and those around you. My mother died aged 50, when I was 24. My father died when I was in my mid-thirties. My best friend died when she was 46, my first spiritual teacher before I was 40. All those people died from various types of cancer.

3

No one persons' grief is greater than any others of course. I list the above only to show that these experiences have all shaped the writing of this book in their own way and that I speak from experience in doing so.

It is said (originally by Benjamin Franklin) that there are two certainties in life - taxes and death. Whilst a great many of us can be fairly sure of the requirement to pay tax, there are people in the world who do not, for different reasons. There is not however, a single person for whom death will not happen and this is just as it should be.

This means that dealing with death, of our loved ones and those we know of, as well as facing and accepting the inevitability of our own, is an important, if not vital, part of the human experience. To this end the grief process becomes an essential part of life and living. It is not something we can ever be cured of as it is not an illness, rather a process. That process, as the wise quote before this introduction tells us, is one of healing. I hope that this book will go some way to helping you with yours.

CHAPTER 1 - THE THERAPEUTIC TAROT

Tarot, when it began, was a game, played largely only by those of sufficient wealth to be able to afford expensive, hand-painted decks, these being the only ones available. Its popularity spread from what is believed to be its origins in northern Italy, across Europe. During the 18th Century French occultists began to research and publish works on the Tarot seeing esoteric connections with all manner of approaches to spirituality. From there the Tarot began to be used for divination, from where it found a massive popularity, spreading hugely in the second half of the 20th Century.

I published the first of my three volumes of 'Tarot Therapy' books in 1990, grandiosely purporting it to be 'Tarot for the new Millennium'! Since then, I am pleased to say that the last twenty years has seen a gradual rise and increase of the use of the Tarot for personal and spiritual development, with many Tarot authors and teachers adding to the value of its use in this light.

Part of the huge popularity of the Tarot over the years could be because there is no-one historical source we can point to as the authoritative guide or rule book that tells us how it should or must be used. It is therefore open to individual theory, interpretation and use. As such we can happily see everything as having something of value to contribute to the 'Tarot archive'. My own contribution, borne simply out of how I first saw and naturally viewed and used the cards, was what I have come to term 'Tarot Therapy'.

The term 'therapy' is used here in a developmental and holistic sense, which is explained further and more specifically below. My approach is in no way suggested to be a better one than anybody else's, or make a claim to be what it was really created for. It is simply the end product of my use of the Tarot over the past 40 years and what I have come to believe and experience as a useful and entirely helpful means to help us deal with issues, whether physical, emotional, mental and/or spiritual.

The structure of the Tarot deck seems to me perfectly suited to this when we look at the construction and operation of the human being, the one reflecting the other. The most accepted and established Tarot decks consist of 78 cards, divided into two parts, known as the Major and Minor Arcana. The term arcana is akin to arcane, in its sense of being hidden, occult, or of a mystery or secret.

In the therapeutic approach the Major Arcana cards are seen as that which affect the whole person, this being holistically 'greater than the sum of the parts'. Those parts form the Minor Arcana, the four suits of the deck, most commonly known as Pentacles, Cups, Swords and Wands. These relate to the different levels of the human being and their realm of influence is best shown in tabular form –

SUIT	ELEMENT	LEVEL
MAJOR ARCANA	SPIRIT/ETHER	WHOLE SELF
WANDS	FIRE	SPIRITUAL
SWORDS	AIR	MENTAL
CUPS	WATER	EMOTIONAL
PENTACLES	EARTH	PHYSICAL

To understand the efficacy of the Tarot in a therapeutic model we need here to enter the world of energy. It is at this point that we enter the realm of the sub-physical, and the spiritual, esoteric, or if you prefer 'woo-woo', level of existence.

In this fabled realm the view is taken that everything that exists does so primarily and formatively at an energetic level. In other words, for anything to exist, it must first do so in an energetic form. This is true whether it be a physical thing - a blade of grass, leaf, tree, raindrop, insect, dog, elephant, or human being – or an action, emotion, thought, or belief. So it is we need to realise that this energy is causal to our reality, at every level. Further, we know that we can effect this energy, and therefore the reality we can experience. We can do this by varied means and methods, and it is here that the Tarot can be utilised to such positive effect.

In the table above we see that each of the suits can be related to one of the four constituent parts of the human being and that the combination of these relates to the energy of the 22 Major Arcana cards which govern the whole human being. When we then add the impact, or outworking of the energy of each of these, we can see the field of influence over which we can have that positive impact in ourselves and lives.

SUIT	ELEMENT	LEVEL	OUTWORKING
MAJOR ARCANA	SPIRIT/ETHER	WHOLE SELF	GROWTH
WANDS	FIRE	SPIRITUAL	BELIEF
SWORDS	AIR	MENTAL	THINKING
CUPS	WATER	EMOTIONAL	FEELING
PENTACLES	EARTH	PHYSICAL	DOING

Over my years of working with the Tarot I have come to see the cards as not 'meaning' anything, in the sense of the interpretations given in the myriad books on this subject. Rather, I see them as an encapsulation and expression of energy, as it is effecting the client or user in that time. Whilst this is particular to that individual and applies only at that time, it can be said that there is a core, or central understanding for each card. In the Minor Arcana, this can be arrived at by combining the influence, or energy of the suit to which it belongs, with its number.

By way of example, we can see that the suit of Cups relates to our emotions and feelings. In traditional numerology, the number 5 can relate to external forces, as well as an upset or perhaps unexpected change. So the appearance of the Five of Cups card could suggest that there are others around the client who are influencing them emotionally, and that those influences may be creating feelings that are upsetting for them.

Whilst this example is somewhat simplistic, it serves to illustrate the principle. In the context of Tarot readings the other cards chosen will all have a bearing and impact on the energies at play for that person. Coupled with the experience, knowledge and intuition of the 'Tarot Therapist' the energies that the cards reveal can be discussed, along with appropriate responses to them.

In the case of the Court cards, the therapeutic model for the Tarot again suggests a combination of two energies as the basic, core concept or energy of the card. Of course we have the influence of the suit the card belongs to, which is combined with a further elemental energy, depending on which court card it is.

The four Court cards of each suit are typically known as Page, Knight, Queen and King, although there are many variations on these, depending on the theme of the deck. It may be easier to think of them as Daughter, Son, Mother and Father respectively. These are archetypal rather than gender specific. These energies and their workings are again best seen in a table –

SUIT	ELEMENT	LEVEL	ENERGY	RESPONSE
PENTACLES	EARTH	PHYSICAL	PRACTICAL	ACTION
CUPS	WATER	EMOTIONAL	FEELING	FEELING
SWORDS	AIR	MENTAL	THOUGHT	THINKING
WANDS	FIRE	SPIRITUAL	BEING	BELIEF

These ascriptions are my own, others choose different alignments. I take the suit as the primary energy affecting the individual, the card being the reaction or response to that. Following the above, the King of Pentacles will first want to act, considering 'what can I do about this'. This is followed by thinking about what he has done - 'what have I learnt about this'. In other words, he learns by doing.

Lastly we have the Major Arcana, the remaining 22 cards of the Tarot deck. The holistic understanding of the human being says that when we combine the four elemental levels, as in the Minor Arcana suits, we arrive at the complete, or whole self. This is the province of the Major cards. They depict energies we experience as a whole. These may be energies that reach deeper within us, have a more profound impact, or opportunity for learning, growth and development. So it is I see them as the 'Soul' level of our being.

It can be important to state that the Major cards are not seen as more important than the Minor, only different in their scope of influence. In the therapeutic model, all cards are seen as having equal importance and validity, just as with the holistic paradigm we take all levels of the self into account.

To come to an understanding of the energies of the Major Arcana cards it is really necessary to either read up about each card individually and/or make your own notes as you study each one. We can however, provide here a layout that allows for some breakdown and structure that serves as a place to begin –

				FOOL			
REALM OF BODY	MAGICIAN	HIGH PRIEST-ESS	EMPRESS	EMPEROR	HIEROPHANT	LOVERS	CHARIOT
REALM OF MIND	STRENGTH	HERMIT	WHEEL	JUSTICE	HANGED MAN	DEATH	TEMPERANCE
REALM OF SPIRIT	DEVIL	TOWER	STAR	MOON	SUN	JUDGEMENT	WORLD

From this table we can see that the first seven cards, The Magician through to The Chariot are concerned with what I call the 'Realm of the Body' – energies that affect our physical path through our life. The middle row of cards relate to the Realm of the Mind as this affects our mental understanding of our self and life. The bottom row shows us the spiritual development and lesson we are learning, or may need to learn as we live our life.

The Fool is seen as the energy of that which simply 'is', the human soul itself, the spark of existence and life that exists within all things. It is energy itself and answers every question with 'why not' or 'because'. He can show us that there is sometimes no reason, things just are; that there is nothing beyond 'it is what it is', and that there is no meaning of life other than life itself.

The cards that follow, numbered 1 to 21, depict the journey or quest taken by The Fool – all of us – as we live our lifetimes (deliberate plural), learning what is required by each of us. This is not done in a linear fashion, despite the numerical sequence. They can be seen as stages in our process of growth, development or awakening, to wholeness.

As mentioned above, the therapeutic approach to the Tarot does not ascribe a meaning to the cards. Rather they are seen as encapsulated, or frozen energy, rather like a still from a film, the film in this case being that of the client or user's life. Each card shows us an energy that is active at the time the card is selected. What is required now is to assess and determine how that energy is having an impact upon the individual and then how they can best respond to that. Put another way, we need to see the inner influence of the card, then the outer; the understanding of it, then the action, or the energy then the response.

Since we are working without a meaning for the card we could begin with a simple description of it: 'We see someone who looks like he is about to walk over the edge of a cliff. He seems to be too busy smelling a flower to see where he is going, and seems oblivious to the dog that is jumping up at him. It looks like a warm, sunny, clear day and we can see the landscape stretching to the distance far below the cliff'.

The reader might then simply ask the client 'what do you make of that, what does it suggest to you'? 'Oblivion' says our client, while another might say 'the bliss of not knowing or needing to know'. In the context of grief this could be very telling, allowing the reader to ask if that is something they are feeling, or perhaps wishes they could. The conversation continues, with further cards being used as required. With certain cards the reader might suggest a number of self-help exercises or actions the card could suggest, to explore their issue further and thereby cause the energy indicated by it to flow, helping the situation progress and evolve in the process.

It is important here to understand that the nature of energy is to flow, to always move. Its very nature does not allow it to be static, any more than we can not breathe, The Universe is not still and is continually evolving. Energy that is not flowing is stuck and in the human being this creates a problem. If we are not expressing our feelings then they remain trapped or locked within us and so seek some other outlet. This is usually in the form of a physical malady, hence the body-mind connection between cancer and grief – and many other conditions of course.

Whilst most easily illustrated with the emotions, this principles applies to all levels of the human being and the energy must flow throughout us and be acted upon if we are to be as healthy and whole as we can be. When working with a number of cards with a client, a predominance of one suit or another can indicate an excess, or build-up of energy at this level, showing a potential blockage of energy there that we need to respond to.

The traditional method of Tarot reading is to use 'Spreads', laying out a certain number of cards in a specified pattern, each card relating to a different area or aspect of the subject that the spread addresses. I have found however that working with the cards as energies and without ascribed meanings means that spreads impose a limit on the response to the card, since it must be interpreted in the context of the placing in the spread, rather than purely as an energy.

So it is that over the years I have evolved a method of reading without a spread and essentially the only structure I have to my readings is that there is no structure! It may be that I ask a client for a number of cards they would like to work with, or fan the entire deck out before them and invite them to pick however many they wish. Or it can be that we simply choose one card, work with that until we feel we are done, then select another, and continue in this way until a natural end point presents itself.

An alternative approach can be that before we turn to the Tarot, we spend some time talking with the client, allowing them to tell us where they are at, what their issue is and they feel they need. We can then use a more diagnostic approach with the cards. Taking into account what the client has said, we might suggest that they need the energy of the Six of Swords, for example. The traditional image of this card is that of a ghost-like figure rowing two people, wrapped in cloaks across a river, the six swords pointing down in the boat.

This might suggest an energy of mentally needing the guidance of someone else, perhaps external to the situation - in the context of grief, a grief counsellor, or volunteer, or perhaps speaking with a friend who is a little removed from the situation, to provide an objective line of thought. This might reveal a way of thinking where the client can begin to look ahead, even if they cannot see this at present (the card is usually depicted at night).

That might lead to the client then picking another card from the remainder of the deck, should they ask a question, or further discussion occurs until the reader then suggests the next card they have diagnosed as the energy needed to best respond to at that time.

Should you prefer to work with a Spread however, that is of course, absolutely fine. Whether arranged as a spread or simply a number of cards taken and arranged in a line, as is my wont, we can see the cards selected as an 'energy map' of the client at that time. This means that we can look for any indications of their energetic condition and required response in such things as:

- Predominance of any suit
- Repetition of numbers
- Court Card occurrences (two Pages etc.)
- Progress of numbers (4,5,6 etc.)
- Grouping of cards (three Majors together etc.)
- Starting and Ending cards (e.g. an Ace to a Ten, two of the same number)

and anything else that strikes you as significant.

Whichever method you choose to work with, I have found that there is usually a focus to be placed on one particular card. There is very often one card in a reading that seems to sum up the issue being dealt with, that 'hits the nail on the head' as so many clients have said to me, and that just demands further attention and work. It is not necessary to go looking for such a card if one does not present itself. I mention this only to show that one card can often be quite enough when working with the depth, attention to detail and sensitivity required when guiding someone through their grief process. A later Chapter gives an outline of a method of working with one card at a time as an ongoing process through grief that is the focus of the book.

CHAPTER 2 – THE GRIEF PROCESS AND THE TAROT

To begin our analysis and method of linking together the grief process with the Tarot I would urge and recommend when dealing with grief (or preferably before), to read the widely acknowledged book by Elisabeth Kubler-Ross and David Kessler 'On Grief and Grieving'.

In this seminal work, along with its predecessor 'On Death and Dying', the process by which we experience and respond to grief is categorized into five stages, which as we shall see, correlate very easily and naturally with the Tarot. This is the basis for how we can work with the Tarot to enable and aid the healing that it ultimately provides.

It should be said at this stage of coming to know and understand the nature and process of grief, that like so much in human nature and experience, it is not logical. As such the five stages do not represent neat and tidy boxes into which each of our feelings, thoughts, instincts and actions which arise as we go through grief, can be placed like some dry mathematical formula.

Nor is the process a linear one, in the sense of moving from one of the five stages to another before we conclude with what is generally seen as the final stage of acceptance. In this it is just like the Tarot. Rather, different things occur for different individuals in different ways and at different times and stages. The nature and means of grief are individual and do not ascribe to any limitation or time. Each thing as it arises needs to be 'faced and embraced' as it does so.

I use the phrase 'face and embrace' deliberately, it being one of those nifty phrases that can be helpful to have in mind. By this I mean the need we have that in order to come to accept something, whatever it might be, we must be able to face it head on and see it for what it really is. It does not mean we come to like or love it, but come to know its reality and ultimately accept it. I have found we need to do this with each of the stages of grief and whatever else life throws at us.

By working with the Tarot we can help to make sense of these things and provide some rationale to our grief process. Perhaps especially because it is not logical or linear, the Tarot is perfectly suited to this work. Those familiar with a therapeutic approach to the Tarot will know the manner in which it can serve to act as a reflection of the inner state, condition and causes of our being. It is at this level that we can engage with ourselves through use of the Tarot in this same therapeutic and energetic way.

In the Kubler-Ross model the five stages of grief are given the classifications that follow.

DENIAL

When we see this classification we immediately think that this is when we tell ourselves 'it is not true' that someone has died, and/or when we refuse to believe or accept it. We can find ourselves almost pretending that everything is just as it was and expect to hear from that person sooner or later.

In my experience it can also run deeper than that. It can be something of a wishful instinct to want to tell ourselves they have not died and we will have contact with them at some point, just as we have always done. And beneath that I have found there is an involuntary response where, try as we might, we cannot convince ourselves that they are dead and we shall not see them again (I will omit continual comments that say 'until we see them in spirit' – you may or may not accept this, but for those that do we'll take it as read). We keep visiting what has happened in our head but it just won't go in. It is not because we don't want to believe it, just that our minds simply cannot comprehend the fact in one fell swoop, it needs to sink in gradually.

I wanted to do this when Laura died as I knew it would help with the pain of the grief. Despite repeatedly giving myself the message that my daughter was dead, it would just not go in, nor would it for her Mum or her sister. I came to realise that trying to make it happen was futile and that it had to occur in its own time, however long that was. Regardless of how much I might want it, I could not make it happen, it would do so naturally and only when the time was right.

This can leave you with a certain numbness that is likened to this stage, in an almost twilight world where nothing seems quite real other than the pain and anguish you feel. Each time you awake there is a few seconds of quiet or peace even, and then the freight train of reality arrives full speed at the station in your head and you soon return to the numb state you went to sleep with.

The repeated refrain of 'I just can't believe it' has a very applicable double-meaning here and can serve to aptly summarise the Denial stage. Belief is not necessarily a logical thing and can come from a level in our minds deeper than the logical, rational operation of the conscious. As such, it takes a certain amount of time, the length of which is different for each person, for the fact of a persons' death to register at the deeper sub-conscious level of our mind.

When and how that happens can also be different for each of us. It may be a definite moment, triggered by some stimulus that allows this recognition and realisation. Or it may be a more gradual thing that we come to uncover after it has happened, even without our consciously knowing, which is the point of course. It may be that we wake one day and something else comes into our mind, and we realise then that the reality train has left that station and we are moving to another.

Until then we can be said to be in the denial stage, not because we are pretending or doing it wrong, but simply because we have to let the full reality of such blows fall by degrees. It is the way our minds work in order to survive and to do so in as healthy and whole a way as possible.

ANGER

Everyone has anger, a temper that at some point will take over our objectivity, and cause us to proceed with words, thoughts, feelings and actions that we would not ordinarily respond to. We all have anger and it is part of the human condition. What matters is how we respond to it and what we do about it. This is not to suggest that we should not have it, deny it or bury it. It is there and as such demands attention and responding to in some way if we are to be healthy and whole.

In the case of grief it can be common for anger to be focused on two things – anger that the death has happened and anger at the person who has died. Both understandable yet both irrational. Either way our anger is an energy that we need to channel and release. If we do not it can nestle somewhere in our being, working away with its corrupting force to cause our lives to follow a pattern we would not otherwise take and not one that leads to our growth and progression.

Anger can surface suddenly, prompted by the loosest of connections or by something obvious and immediate. It can be helpful to recognize our own particular triggers and why we might have them, as well as how to respond to them healthfully. The Tarot can help here.

Anger can also be a more consistent state of being, almost as if it were a persona, a state of being that we have adopted as a result of our grief. It may be that we can only see the world as a cruel place of pain and loss or that the death of our loved one is simply so unfair, especially so

17

when those who are murderers or some such still live. In this way anger can be an unfocussed thing, just something inside us we find is there.

It can be that this ultimately defensive stance is one we find ourselves adopting, not because we have chosen to but because it is a means of survival, of getting by whilst the loss is too hard to 'face and embrace'. When we are ready the hardness of the anger can soften and we are able to reclaim our natural way of being.

It is my strong belief, and experience, that the vast majority of people are good and that love is the natural tendency and instinct of all people. The rest are layers we acquire through our lives and our experiences and are part of the natural process of living. Anger is one of those layers, and a very powerful one, yet beneath that is a love that supports all that we are and do, feel, think and believe. That is how strong it is.

BARGAINING

There is nothing we can do about death. It gets us all in the end. Therefore it is inevitable that we will experience the death of someone we love in our lives. It is just a matter of the manner of that death and how we respond to it. This does not stop us engaging in some bargaining however, whether before or after the death.

One of the easiest and strongest ways to recognise this is when we do the 'what if's'. In the case of being close to someone who is dying we can help ourselves to deal with this scenario by considering what if they had/had not done/said this, or what if I had/had not done/said that. They or we did or did not do or say whatever it was and so we know it is pointless to consider it now, but we still do it.

It can help our minds to process and absorb the stark reality of the situation we are faced with by considering possibilities and alternatives. This way we can convince ourselves that there was or is no other way than to accept what is happening, or has happened. It is rather like knowing that we have tried, or at least thought, everything we possibly can before we must then accept the truth of the situation. We knew it all along of course, but we are such that we need to go through this process, or put ourselves through it, to find a place of being 'at peace' with it.

We can find that we repeat these scenarios in our minds many times over, like being trapped in a revolving door in our head. This can be because the energy of the grief, preparatory or resultant, needs an outlet and must find some expression. This may be in the form of these repeating thought patterns but also having the same conversation many times, with anyone who will listen, or we make listen! Each time we do so, the energy is lessened and loosened a bit, and we feel a little better.

DEPRESSION

Of course when someone we love, or just someone we know or even just hear about, dies, it is very sad. Arguably, it can be more so in tragic, sudden, unexpected or criminal circumstances. And yet, for the person that has died, it is fine. This view may be dependent on your spiritual beliefs, but the majority of spiritual belief systems or traditions tell us the personal that has died continues and that any suffering, on any level, does not.

So we are not sad for them, but for the dead person's loved ones and most of all, for ourselves. We should not have any guilt about this, as it is perfectly natural. The measure of the sadness and how we experience it is an individual thing. For some the loss is (almost) unbearable, the weight of it pressing down upon us so heavily we may not even be able to drag ourselves out of bed for some time. For others they may attend a funeral and shed some tears, but once done the sadness is attended to and they continue with their life.

This does not mean that the sadness is any bigger, deeper or more acute for one than the other, only that we experience it in different ways. We need to give ourselves permission to be sad and express this as we need to. There can be times and places where it is not really appropriate, but others where it most certainly is. Our need is to recognise our sadness and our loss and allow ourselves to keep releasing that energy, until we are done and a sense of something we might call peace begins to be felt.

My personal view, and my experience, is that people can think that they are being weak because they keep getting upset or crying after the death of someone they love. Yet I believe the opposite to be true. It takes strength, courage and personal power to open ourselves and our hearts to the pain of the loss, the devastating sadness that keeps welling up within that we just cannot stop. It may be easier to create a barrier of defence or pretense that we are ok but ultimately it can be a weakness of fear that causes us to do this.

Of course some people may have a need to tell themselves they are not sad like they really are for a while until they feel ready to admit they are and engage with it. Again, it is an individual process and one approach is no better or worse than any other, they are just different. Our need is to do what works for us.

I am addressing here the emotion of sadness rather than any level or type of clinical depression. The dividing line may be a thin one at times but it can be vital to recognise when we may be in need of professional help, in whatever form is right for us and seek this as each person requires.

As we embrace the seemingly bottomless pit of our sadness and loss so we can find a way through that darkness until one day, awake early yet again, we witness the sunrise and see and sense it reflected, in however tiny a way, within us.

ACCEPTANCE

It can be easy to think when someone dies that at some stage we can, will or should 'get over it'. That is a fallacy however. That person will always be dead and nothing can make it better again. We will never get to a place where we like it and our lives return to what they were, as if nothing has changed.

The point is that something has changed and that cannot be reversed. So although we cannot get over it in that way we can reach a place where we accept it, by which is meant we can feel a sense of peace once again. This of course takes time and how long is, once more, an individual thing. It is usually a gradual process rather than something we simply wake up with one day.

The gradual movement to a sense of inner peace is one that can happen without our noticing until after it has occurred. There can be stages with this, such as when we suddenly realise we have not thought about the person who has died, or anything relating to it, for a time, and we immediately feel guilty. Gradually as this happens more, we feel less guilt until we can even sense pleasure in something. That can be followed with a thought that our loved one would have enjoyed this too, and rather than sadness, the sense is more nostalgic, and then, quietly, timidly, but perceptively, comes acceptance.

We cannot make ourselves accept the loss of someone, it is something that has to, and can only, happen in whichever way is right for each person and in whatever time it needs to. It is rather like the way in which the waves of a sea do not suddenly become calm after a storm, but little by little, wave by wave, they are lessened until eventually, and at last, it is calm again.

Indeed we experience our grief very much in waves too. In the early days after a death we are shattered into myriad pieces and can think and feel we can never be whole again. Yet over time, piece by piece, we can create a new self, different perhaps than before, but no less complete and even perhaps, stronger, more understanding, tolerant, compassionate and progressive in our self and life than before.

PREPARATORY GRIEF

Alongside these five stages of Grief there is also what is known as Preparatory Grief, sometimes called Anticipatory Grief. This is most commonly seen as applying to the dying person or those with a terminal illness and their process of coming to terms with this. The majority of references currently refer to the patient themselves, yet in my experience this can also be applied to those close to or caring for a loved one who has a terminal diagnosis, or a condition that necessitates a drastic change in life-style.

We can experience Grief before the ultimate focus or event of what that Grief is about actually happens. This is Preparatory Grief. The way in which this may be done depends to a large extent on the individual and their circumstances. It may be a largely inner process, whether for the dying person or the loved one. Whether the individual is able or willing to discuss their Grief process with another, professional or friend, may govern this.

I have found that the five stages outlines above apply in the same way for Preparatory Grief. This is for myself as a 'carer' in the situation Amy and I have as we negotiate her cancer diagnosis, treatment and 'progression' if that word can be used here. I can imagine and suppose that it is quite different when faced with our own death, but again, each person is different. Facing our own death is perhaps the ultimate fear we must all face, but to be confronted with this directly, when we know it is going to happen in days/weeks/months is a very different reality to an abstract 'one day' scenario the majority of us have.

What I do know however, is that this is an area that requires more exploration, and especially so for the loved ones of the dying. Grief is ultimately a healing process and this also applies to Preparatory Grief. It can make the transitory process an experience easier to bear for both the dying person and their loved one.

For me, the Tarot is ideally placed for this. It can speak directly to us on the requisite inner level. It is able to directly communicate with us on those dark, inexpressible, secret thoughts and feelings that we do not like to admit to, but that we all have one way or another, when it comes to death and dying. By using the Tarot we need only communicate that which we choose to, knowing that we are not shying away from anything, or avoiding it.

In the next Chapter I would recommend the process of 'Tarot Mentoring' that I have given for the stages of Grief, for working with Preparatory Grief also.

THE FIVE STAGES AND THE TAROT

As with all things Tarot, how these five stages of grief are aligned with the deck is really a matter of personal preference and opinion. There being no rule book when it comes to what can/cannot be done with the Tarot, we are free to place our own approaches and workings on it. So what I offer here is done in this regard and spirit and does not claim to be any authoritarian dictate in any way.

That there are five now recognized stages to the grief process falls rather nicely into our lap when it comes to alignment with the Tarot. There are of course four suits of the Minor Arcana plus the Major Arcana, to which we can ascribe one each of the stages. It is then only a matter of which is which, and this is where your own opinion and approach is what really matters most.

This may be dependent on which deck you work with and so which suit aligns to which Element, or the background of any tradition you are schooled in and work with, to align with their particular teachings. None can be emphatically claimed as wrong. I would suggest that you be clear about why you have chosen your ascriptions though, and are sure that it works for you.

As before, the stages I use where are easiest shown in a table, followed with a description for each. For this I have repeated the first table from Chapter 1, with the addition of the Grief column.

SUIT	ELEMENT	LEVEL	GRIEF
MAJOR ARCANA	SPIRIT/ETHER	WHOLE SELF	ACCEPTANCE
WANDS	FIRE	SPIRITUAL	ANGER
SWORDS	AIR	MENTAL	DENIAL
CUPS	WATER	EMOTIONAL	DEPRESSION
PENTACLES	EARTH	PHYSICAL	BARGAINING

It is perhaps worth a reminder here that the stages are not seen as being experienced in any kind of linear order, or indeed one at a time until we reach completion. Indeed the whole concept of a completion when it comes to Grief is, I think, and in my experience, a misnomer. This is in the sense that we never get over the death of a loved one and it is all ok again. Rather we come to terms with the loss and accept it, as with what is generally seen as the 'final' stage, that of Acceptance.

Again, getting to that place is something of a dance, and not a process of logic that fits into neat little boxes, contrary to the table above! Our natural tendency is to flit about from one stage to another as we, initially at least, struggle and strive to 'get our heads around' what has happened, 'work it all out', 'process the loss' and 'move on with our lives'. The experience of grief for most people, and certainly for myself, is that some days are better than others.

The process can be rather like when we are expecting a baby, or someone close to us is - everywhere we look we see pregnant women, babies, and anything and everything is to do with pregnancy, birth and babies! When we are experiencing grief, it seems that everywhere there are reminders of death and the person who has died. We could see this as just a psychological reaction to these things – we are not actually experiencing any more of them than we usually do, it is simply that we are more aware of those that are there because that is where our mind is focused. Equally, we could see this process as the Universe doing what it does to help us shift to a place of acceptance and integration with our new circumstances and situation. Perhaps the truth is that it is some of both.

So it is we place the five stages of grief with the Tarot in a generalised manner only. I have found in choosing cards to help my own grief process that cards from each of the suits or the Major Arcana, did belong in the stage to which I have given them. This not only helped me deal with my grief, it also helped me engage actively with life, offering me a way forward at times when I needed one.

I also found that the cards I chose worked at two levels at different times - that of explaining what was going on inside me and that of giving me strategies to focus on and use. It can be very helpful to consider what need within you each card may be suggesting, in terms of how you can best respond to what you sense about it. So in our therapeutic model of the Tarot we see the card as a reflection of an aspect of our inner energy and then consider what our best response to that can be to process, release or express it.

Here are the Tarot ascriptions I make with the five stages.

PENTACLES - BARGAINING

The suit of Pentacles, or sometimes Coins, is traditionally connected to all things practical – as the very first book about Tarot that I read ('Tarotmania' by Jan Woudhuysen) said 'if you can point to it, or hold it in your hand, it comes under Pentacles'. In fortune-telling or divinatory use Pentacles cards when they appear are said to be to do with work, finance, home, health and material possessions.

For me, working as I do with a more therapeutic approach to the Tarot, Pentacles is to do with what we are doing with our selves and lives. I see it as the manifestation of the physical energy of our being i.e. how what is within us causes us to actually do what we do. These cards are the province of our physical selves, the actions we take and also the outworking or reflection, of our higher, spiritual level in the everyday world. In terms of how we can best respond to them, these cards can show us our needs on a physical level.

When these cards appear for you during your grief process, they can relate to the Bargaining stage. The simplest and most immediate way to place this suit with this stage is that we use money – Coins or Pentacles – to bargain for the things we want – if I give you this much money will you give me that thing or do this for me. In terms of working with the Tarot here what can be helpful to be aware of is what need we may have at this level and what outcome we may be wanting from our bargaining.

It can also be helpful to consider what or who the focus of our Bargaining is. It may be with the Universe (Goddess, God or whatever deity/deities you work with), situations or circumstances that relate to the death we have experienced, the person who has died, those around us, or of course, ourselves. In seeking to make our bargains it is the remedy that we seek that can tell us more about what we need and these cards can guide us to this.

CUPS - DEPRESSION

Traditionally Cups speak of our relationships and the people in our lives. Our relationships all hinge on feelings, within each person involved in that relationship and those shared between them.

As can be seen from the above table, therapeutically speaking Cups cards show us the energy of the feelings in our being. They speak of our emotional energies and how we need to respond to them. When we draw a card from the suit of Cups it can be guiding us to look to how we are feeling and what is happening for us at this level at that time.

The expression of our emotions is a vital thing to maintain health and well-being. Emotion that is not expressed lies still and can become buried within us, sometimes for many years, quietly doing damage to what and who we are. Whilst it can be important to seek appropriate outlets, what is necessary is that we release our feelings. This requires of course that we must first acknowledge what we are feeling and 'own up to it', since some feelings are ones we would rather not have. Again, we need to 'face and embrace' them if we are to deal with them. Simply put, if we do not want them, we need to release them and this is what these cards can show us.

Whilst dictionary definitions of Depression talk about a mental state and mental health, when we look at explanations of depression, the terminology is of feeling and mood, with emotions such as 'being low', guilt, sadness, and 'being tearful' commonly cited. It is for this reason that Cups cards are aligned with the Depression stage of Grief.

It is easy to think of someone who is depressed as being 'down all the time' and 'feeling sorry for themselves', with a need to 'snap out of it'. Fortunately with a more modern and one would hope enlightened awareness of depression, what it is and what causes it, such concepts are becoming archaic. Rather we can see someone experiencing depression as simply dealing with an experience they are having.

This can of course be a common thing when we have recently experienced the death of someone we love or are close to. All kinds of feelings can well up from within, and from without. We can find our thoughts turn to the death we have experienced in our life as soon as we wake each day and before we know it we are crying and miserable. We may be carrying out our day and something happens that reminds us, directly or otherwise, of the one who has died and we are back feeling sad, lost, and miserable and so on.

Negotiating these feelings can be like swimming against a strong current that just keeps coming, wave after wave. When Cups cards appear for us we find that they can guide us upstream to where the going is calmer, through understanding the undercurrents that cause the waves.

SWORDS - DENIAL

The suit of Swords can sometimes be seen and labelled as the 'negative' suit. The cards can sometimes show unpleasant images and can look as if they depict 'doom and gloom' by various methods. This for me, and especially so in the therapeutic context and approach, is a complete error.

In following the therapeutic based model I work with, Swords cards are expressions of the mental level of the human being, our mental processes and needs, what is going on in our minds and the impact of our thoughts and thinking on our being.

The approach of fortune-telling tells us that Swords are to do with communication, which can come in all kinds of ways, and travel. As such this is not so far removed from our therapeutic view, only that the letter is more internally focused than the former.

In following the approach that the cards are nothing more or less than energy, and as such ideally suited to using them for developmental and therapeutic means, it can be important to see and respond to the images in the Tarot deck at much more than just face value. This can be especially so in the case of this suit. If we take for example the typical depiction of the Three of Swords, this cards' standard image is that of the three Swords piercing a large red heart.

In my experience as soon as this is seen by a client they immediately, and justifiably, see it as something bad that is going to hurt them one way or another. However, if we see the Swords as symbols of our mental energy, and the heart typically relating to our feelings, we can see that this can indicate a conflict between the head and heart, where the client's head may be telling them one thing, the heart another. In other words, what is being thought or focused on mentally may be creating emotional hurt and pain.

Since three is a creative energy and force, we can see a need and a potential for using our thoughts to help rather than hinder our process. It may be that we need to be more objective about our approach. We can become aware of what our feelings are and if, as they very often are, they are a result of what we are thinking. Once realised we can be enabled to free ourselves from a destructive or limiting thought pattern and move toward something more constructive and helpful.

With regard to the Denial level of the grief process, it can be argued that this mostly or predominately happens in our heads. In terms of my daughter, her death just did not seem real, I could not get it through my head, as the saying goes, that she was dead, for some time after it happened. I knew in my heart it was real and I most certainly felt this, but despite my telling myself repeatedly it was true, still my mind refused to accept it. Perhaps this is why we can have the recreated experience at various unexpected times of the realisation hitting us, when we wake each day and when our thoughts or focus has been elsewhere for a time.

It can take us time and simple repetition of the fact for us to reach the point where our minds finally do believe the death has happened and to accept it as a reality. It is only by replaying the event in our minds that it can sink below the conscious thoughts to a deeper level where we 'know' it is real, true and fact. The Swords cards can help us find our way through this maze.

WANDS - ANGER

With this suit we enter the realm of the Fire element and all that this brings. Traditionally this is translated as being the creative and inspirational aspect, as well as our beliefs, drive, ambition, enthusiasm (or lack of it) and that inner force that makes us get up in the morning.

For our purposes here, Wands cards are related to the stage of Anger in the grief process. This can be where the 'red mist' of the Fire descends and we find ourselves just angry. We may not be aware that our anger is because someone has died, we may simply feel a force that comes out as anger. This may be by way of increased frustration, short-temperedness, complaining about things we would normally not be bothered by, lack of patience and many other ways that this energy seeks its way out from within us.

For many people, we do not like to feel anger and so it can be easy to want to suppress it. However, the energy of anger is a powerful one and like all levels of energy we have explored, it needs to be expressed if we are to remain as healthy and whole as we need to be, and learn to come to terms with the death we have experienced.

It can also be difficult for us to know what we are angry about specifically. Whilst we know we may be angry because our loved one has died, we may not have an exact focus for it – it may be because of the manner of their death, what we did or did not do before it happened, what they did or did not do, what others did or did not do and so on. We may be angry at God, the Universe or whatever for 'allowing' it to happen, the unfairness and injustice of it, the ongoing impact of it for those left behind, and so on.

There can be a great many things to be angry about when someone dies, when we begin to think about it. They are all quite understandable and yet very few may be actually rational, especially in view of it being the one and only true certainty of life, as we saw at the beginning of this book. I have found it can be more helpful just to accept that I have anger, which in itself is a somewhat different thing than saying 'I am angry'.

Our anger is justified though, because we have it. What perhaps matters more is that we recognise it and express in a way that is not destructive, to ourselves or others. This is where the Wands cards can act as wise counsellors, helping us see more of what is happening within us at this level and in this way.

MAJOR ARCANA - ACCEPTANCE

The twenty-two cards of the Major Arcana are typically seen as depicting the larger 'life-lessons' we are each here to learn through our various lifetimes. They are seen as stages of unfoldment on the path to wholeness, or psychological 'individuation', the means by which we can reach enlightenment, and the various archetypal identities of the self which we must come to know and understand.

In the holistic approach to the structure of the Tarot used in this book and in my Tarot work generally, the Major Arcana energies are those which affect the whole of our being. We can view them as the result of combining the four other energies and levels of the self, the product of this being 'greater than the sum of the parts'. This 'whole self' is the province and scope of the Major Arcana cards.

In terms of the grief process we can see that the Major cards are likened to the stage of Acceptance. This is usually seen as the last stage of the process, when we reach the point at which we come to a place where we accept it is real, will not be fixed and have made whatever adjustments we need to as a result, We have already made the point that it is not something we achieve when everything is ok again and we have 'got over it'.

The death of a loved one can be the most profound of experiences we are ever likely to have in our lives and is one we cannot shy away from, or pretend will not or has not happened. As such it is something about which we simply have to accept, somehow, one way or another. The energy here reaches, and needs to reach, to the very deepest level of ourselves, the core and foundation of our being, and that which makes us who we are.

When we reach a point of being able to accept and in some way 'make peace with' the fact and experience of a death, we can be said to have learned the lesson the Major cards can be showing us as they occur. The experience I have had with the Major cards through my grief is that they can be rarer in their appearance than is usual, but when they do they require attention in a different way to the suit cards. This may require meditation and reflection or other work specific to the challenge we may be struggling with, which invariably seems to be the case.

It can be important and helpful to remember that as we do indeed work though and learn to 'face and embrace' these struggles, through the despair, rants, tears, agony and solitude, we are always, little by little, breath by breath, thought by thought, feeling by feeling and action by action, slowly, ever so slowly, moving inexorably towards that point of acceptance where the death we have experienced no longer seems to dominate or control us.

We can come to acceptance, and peace.

CHAPTER 3 - HOW TO USE THE TAROT FOR THE GRIEF PROCESS

The process I am sharing here is what I used when using the Tarot to help me process my own grief and what I found the most helpful. As you will see, it does not use Spreads but instead focusses on an ongoing process of card selection that does not use anything 'scripted' or pre-assigned in any way.

This approach can require a good awareness of ones' own intuition or instinct and sometimes a certain amount of restraint. What is given is done so in the manner of an outline or basic structure for you to use, and adapt according to your individual needs and wants. As before, there are no prescribed rights or wrongs with the Tarot so you are free to experiment and diversify as much as you wish.

When I began working with the Tarot I did so like everyone else, using the Spreads given in the few Tarot books I had at that time. It became clear that when one read the Tarot, it was done so using a Spread that told you how it should be done. As I progressed it became clear that some spreads worked better for certain questions or subjects, and like most Tarot readers of my profession, as it was by then, I had my preferences as to which Spreads I used.

As I gained more experience and confidence I felt a disquiet about the Spreads I was using, wanting them to include the more holistic approach to the human being that I was learning about, as well as the inner, quantum world of energy. I therefore devised some of my own Spreads for this, some of which are featured in the first volume of my 'Tarot Therapy' books. These enabled me to tap into what I felt was a deeper and more appropriate use of the Tarot and the way I was now working.

However, as I continued I began to feel restrained by the Spreads I was using. Because I had to blend the way I was interpreting a card to its place in the Spread I found that I perceived and wanted to say things that did not fit this prescriptive way of working. I experimented and in the end came to work without using spreads at all.

My method was to allow the client to select however many cards they felt was right for them for their reading. This allows for free reign in how we respond to them and what we do with them through the reading. We are free to move them around, rather than having to stick to the placement on a spread. This yielded some surprising and powerful effects, which can really help a client see the potential and power in the cards, for them to tap into and use.

This has since become my standard method of reading with clients when I do so. I use the term 'with' rather than 'for' deliberately, since it is a dual thing, an exchange, rather than my talking at the client. We work together to uncover and understand the energy of the cards and how this can best be responded to and worked with for them and in their particular situation.

With this method – which I call simply Reading Without Spreads – and which I have detailed elsewhere – it became quite common for there to be one card that seemed to stand out in the reading. This may be because it seemed to summarise the whole reading in itself, and/or that it was clearly the one that needed focusing on and working with more than any other to achieve the required goal for the client.

This card was often identified by the client, whether they knew it or not. As I worked with them through each card they selected, they would often make some kind of exclamation as soon as they saw it, or when I said something about it. Very often I heard a phrase such as 'you've hit the nail on the head', 'that sums it up', or simply, 'that's it'! I would take note of which card this was and return to it at the end of the reading process and suggest this was the primary focus needed, along with some suggestions for work they could do in response. It was and is always so wonderful to receive feedback of what has happened for them since.

TAROT MENTORING

The process I outline here for working with Grief was borne from that single card focus. I have come to call it Tarot Mentoring for it is really allowing the Tarot to become our mentor for this time and purpose.

Mentoring has been defined as the influence or guidance of a mentor, this in turn being someone who supports and encourages others to manage their own learning so that they maximize their own potential. It supports and guides rather than tells us what to do. The way I like to put it is that it is 'helping you to help yourself'.

In this method we work with one card at a time. First we need to select that card and this I have found, is an important thing to be done with due regard for its role. Rather than casually grabbing a deck and pulling out a card, we take a little time over the activity.

My suggestion is first to select your deck – this is if you have more than one and in my experience most Tarot practitioners end up owning more, from a few to hundreds! Different decks can appeal at different times for different reasons and with Grief particularly, it can be good to be open to these promptings from within. It may be that the deck you choose is simply because it is bright and you need a lift that day; it could be the artwork was a style the deceased person may have liked; perhaps you know that person owned this deck too, or even that it was their deck. Whatever reason you have for using that deck, be open to first sensing which one feels right for you to use, each time you do so.

It can then be good to just sit with your deck for a short time. This does not have to be a full meditation session – unless you want to of course – personally in my grief I was much too preoccupied to be able or want to focus on meditating – the irony being that this is precisely the time when it can be so good to do! It is really just a matter of calming one's self and mind from the tumult of thoughts and emotions that can swirl about us at these times. I would suggest closing your eyes, and holding your deck in your hands, take three deeper, slower breaths – breathe in through the nose and out through the mouth if possible, and hold each breath for a moment or two if you can. This will help slow your physical, emotional and mental processes down a little and enable you to have that sense of taking a little time out for yourself.

Once more connected to yourself in this way you are better able to gain a sense of what feels right for you and be more open to and receptive of your intuition and its promptings. You can breathe in that measured way for as long as you wish, and when you feel ready, shuffle the cards. This can be done by whatever method is easiest for you, but do take time to do this reasonably thoroughly. I find that the time spent shuffling the deck allows for a deeper connection, with both the cards and myself within and the greater Universe without – increasing my sense of awareness of and connection to them.

While you are shuffling, or if you prefer while you are doing the above breath work practice, it can help to ask your question, or frame your subject, or at the very least, become aware of what you are choosing your card for. To do this, it is really just a matter of concentrating on it for a time – I find that while shuffling is the perfect time, but I am practiced enough to be able to shuffle without looking at what I am doing and dropping the cards!

Holding your question or subject in mind is what creates an energy flow that will allow the right card for you to emerge. This is all part of the mystery of the Tarot, how the right cards appear, but after 40 years I can say that they absolutely do! Whether we see that or not may be another matter, and this is not blind faith but measured choice.

Equally the principle works that if we do not ask, we do not get. This means that if we have nothing specific we wish or need to know about or feel we need, then we can simply allow the Tarot, or the Universe, to guide us to what we need. I have also found that this works very effectively. In Grief, it can easily be the case that we have no clue as to what we need, and the Tarot is perfectly equipped to show us.

I tend to avoid specific questions, and certainly those that would be answered with a yes/no response or that would tell me what to do or not do. If for instance I was feeling desperately sad about the loss I might ask for a card to show me how best to respond to this. Or it might be that I was acutely aware of something I did regularly with that person and did not know what to do about that now. In this case I would ask for a card to help me deal with this. There are times with grief when all that is just too much, and your question or subject might only be 'help', which is fine and is in fact what I began the process with that gave rise to this book.

When we feel ready it is then a matter of selecting the card from the deck. This may sound trivial but it can be important to have a process which does not allow for any doubt to creep into your mind about the card that you are given being the right one. A set way of working also helps to develop a connection with the whole process, thereby allowing the inner senses to be able to guide you more coherently.

The method I use is to fan out the cards, face down, with a swoop of my hand, across my desk, cloth or just the floor, depending where I am. This takes a bit of practice to become a smooth thing, but just keep doing it repeatedly and you will find a smooth distribution of the cards in a nice arc soon becomes the norm. When doing this I invariably find that there is a break in that arc somewhere along the line, and so I select the card at that break – it is as if the cards are showing me the one I need to have.

Sometimes it is the case that a card is slightly raised or lowered away from the rest in the arc and so stands out. When this happens this is the one I will choose. It can also be that my eyes alight on one card for apparently no reason but I can sense within myself that this is the card I need to have, so I do. You may be one of those people that can sense energy within your hand and so slowly run your hands over the deck, choosing the card when you feel the necessary energetic response. Or you could simply close your eyes, stretch out your hand and pick a card at random.

Then turn over your card and sit with it. I have found that it is our first, initial responses that can be the most telling and relevant, so do take the time to do this. Just hold the card in your hand and be aware of what occurs for you. This can mean the things that pop into your head, as well as emotional reactions to the card and what you see on it, odd 'associations' that come up for you, whether you understand them or not, or whether they seem to have any relevance to the subject at hand. Be conscious too of any physical or bodily sensations that happen. It can be surprising how visceral our responses to cards can be, especially if we have truly taken the time to follow the above process through. Do not worry about logic at all, just be aware of what comes up for you, on any and every level.

Now write those things down, or type them up – I find that I can type closer to my speed of thought than I can write these days. It may be that to begin with you just need to write down a few keywords, things that you know will prompt you when you come back to it and add in the details you want. Allow yourself to express all that comes to you and all that you need to, in whatever way feels right. If you prefer, you can speak about the card and record yourself – most pc and mobile 'phones have a voice recorder now that is simple to operate.

When doing this I encourage you to give free reign to your expression. You may also find yourself wanting to draw something, or perhaps a song comes to mind that you feel expresses the card for you (this is a favourite of mine – I find it really helps express the energy of the card). It could be there is a quote from a poem, line from a play, scene from a film – or a whole film, or anything at all that the card and what you are getting from it brings up for you.

Indulge yourself with it, whatever it is. If it is a film, watch it, play the song as much as you like, sing it, recite the poem and so on. This is all about allowing yourself to respond to the card and record all that it prompts from within you. It does not matter if this seems to veer off topic and seemingly away from anything connected to your grief entirely. Working this way can allow for those things that may not be logically and consciously connected to our grief, but have become buried or lain dormant, perhaps for many years, and here there is a chance for them to emerge into the light, find expression and grant us the invaluable gift of release. When we do so, we feel better about ourselves and lighter – because we are no longer carrying around the energy of what we have rid ourselves of.

There can be an almost unlimited number of things that a card can prompt us with or that can surface for us. As before, there are no rights or wrongs, so give yourself permission to go with whatever happens for you. If you find that you feel blocked or nothing much seems to be happening when you look at your card, you can begin with just describing the card – e.g. "there is a man who has his right arm in the air which is holding a wand and his left hand is down, one finger pointing at the Earth".

This might lead to a thought process – "maybe this is telling me that (the deceased) has crossed over to the other side (or whatever term you wish) and is acknowledging this to me. Maybe I need to acknowledge that in myself". This might lead to a need to sit, talk to the dead person and tell them that you know they have crossed now, and perhaps offer them blessings for their onward journey. Maybe there is an action you need to take for this too, lighting a candle daily for them for a month or whatever feels good. This somewhat random example just came to me as I typed out the start of my description of The Magician, just to illustrate the free form association used.

It can be helpful to then leave what we have written or recorded alone for the remainder of that day, or a couple of days. This allows for those initial responses to seep into us to a deeper level where they can ferment a little and possibly start to produce further realisations and offerings. I have also found it helpful to read back over what I have produced after a day or two and this can also allow for more to emerge from within me that I may not have got otherwise.

It can be important not to go looking for more and more information from a card, but to simply be open to what it gives us and receive it in humility and grace. If that is one simple piece of information or thought then so be it; that is enough. We may need to be very gentle with our tender selves, especially early in the grief process. At times such as these we can feel so damaged and torn apart that we may cling to anything we can get hold of so the appropriate attitude is needed. Be loving to yourself.

Next in the Tarot Mentoring process is placing the card where we will see it. This again, like so much with the Tarot, is personal choice. If you maintain an altar in your home then you may like to place it there. You might prefer to place it on your bedroom mirror - this being somewhere most of us look at least once a day! Perhaps your desk is the perfect place, especially if you work from home. Maybe you consider the fridge to be a great place, and can secure the card using fridge magnets of your choice! If you do not wish to use the card itself, it can quite easily these days be re-created on a pc and printed on a card. If you are creating a physical journal of your Tarot Grief process this gives you an ideal way of illustrating it when you are finished with each card.

If you are concerned about the card getting damaged while it is out, you could always place it in a photo frame, just replacing it with the next card and so on. I have a small, clear Perspex stand in which I slide my cards and which lives on my desk. This keeps my cards safe and allows for me to see it clearly, whilst being quite prominent. It is as I write, next to a photo of my daughter.

It is then a matter of how long you keep that card out for. As before, there is no hard and fast rule for this; in fact there is no rule at all! I have found that the process of grief has no logic and certainly no time awareness or regularity. What I found mattered most was moving with my grief, and therefore choosing the next card when it felt right, or if something has changed or a feeling was particularly prevalent, I was feeling lost, feeling nothing at all or simply because I wanted some sense of something happening to help me with it all.

Given the above wide-ranging list, it may be easy to think that one may as well simply choose a card each day. However this is something I am not an advocate of generally, and not for the grief process. The idea with taking a card to help us with our grief is about connecting with what is happening within us and how to best respond to that. This requires an attitude and approach to the process that is deeper and more meaningful than 'what card will I get today'. Each card taken is more of an event than that, a staging post in the land we travel through that we call Grief. It cannot be cheapened or treated as trite in anyway. Rather it requires that inner connection to the self, the Tarot and the Universe, as described before.

You are your own best judge for when you choose your next card. I have found that by simply being open to the process my natural desire to want to keep working through my grief gave me the inner prompts when needed. If they did not happen, after a few days I became aware in my mind that I had not taken a card for a while and so considered what was going on for me and whether I wished to select the next card. It really comes down to letting it happen naturally, and perhaps employing a certain amount of trust until you get going and the habit is established.

I do recommend keeping a journal of some kind, of your process. This need not be a huge, lengthy thing so it does not become a chore. It can if you wish, be simply a list of the cards you took and the date. You can of course be as creative as you like, including images of your card and anything you feel is relevant for you. This can also be done either in electronic or physical form.

I found that noting the card, date, which deck I was using, and the suit/Major Arcana was helpful, along with my responses to the card. I did not monitor the length of what I wrote at all, but most came in at less than a page of typing. It can be good to be open to adding thoughts or reflections that occur to you while you have that card and are viewing it from its vantage point.

It can be of significant interest and help to plot a table or chart of which of the stages of grief your cards come from. This could show you that you have far more of one stage than another, or that one occurs at more or less regular intervals. Other traits may also emerge that you may otherwise be unaware of. The information you glean from this may show you a need to focus on something you are only dimly aware of in the recesses of your mind or the darkness of your sadness. This may help to bring it up and forwards to a place where it can be more easily identified and responded to. Please refer to the end of Chapter 5 where I share my own process and present the table suggested here, and my response to what it reveals, which is quite amazing.

How long we continue working this way is again an individual thing. Grief is something that we can say is never truly finished, in the sense of 'getting over it' and it is done. Things can occur years later that can cause a reaction within us and allow another expression of our grief to need to be released. Again, it is perhaps the best approach to be open to whatever you need to do.

In the early stages of our grief things can shift fairly quickly and we may find a need to be selecting cards at a fairly rapid rate. As time moves on it may be that this calms more and it becomes something we do less often, but is a no less meaningful part of our process because of this. We can also hit pockets where our grief seems stronger, Christmas being an obvious example, which may require cards to be drawn in quick succession for a week or more.

It may be that we consider our grief never ends and so may feel we want to just continue our Tarot Mentoring. At some point the reason we select our cards may undergo a subtle change and dealing with our grief is no longer our primary reason or purpose. We may or may not be aware of this, and either is fine.

I am not a fan of giving complete readings for oneself, whether using spreads or conducting a complete reading. I feel we cannot be truly objective and will always colour

our interpretation of the cards, knowingly or otherwise. The more subtle level of reading that comes from the links between cards and deeper layers within them is not something best achieved by the self. This is different to working with one card at a time and allowing ourselves to respond to it.

This Tarot Mentoring approach is something I do promote and encourage use of for ourselves however, as an ongoing process of self-awareness, development and healing, as well as increasing our experience and knowledge of the Tarot for others, if we engage in this.

This is summed up with one of my favourite Tarot maxims: 'Life teaches you about Tarot and Tarot teaches you about life'. May the lessons in your Grief guide you well.

CHAPTER 4 - TAROT FOR GRIEF

I am very much an advocate for not sticking to defined 'meanings' for the cards, preferring instead an open, discursive approach, that works with or alongside a client when reading for others. When working with the cards for the self my approach is an immediate, intuitive one, which has been mentioned in the previous Chapter, but to recap involves writing down or recording our first impressions and whatever comes to us on any level, when we first view a card. This is then developed by making further associations when we review what we first came up with and seeing where it leads.

Although I suggest that the cards do not have structured meanings, instead being representations of an inner energetic state or circumstance, it can be argued that they do have a central core, or essence, from which we can develop our individual understanding, each time we select a card, and that may differ from, or extend that core each time.

It is in this spirit that I give what follows for each card; not as something for you to look up when that card appears and assume this is what it means for you, but as a starting or jumping off point for you to work with. I have written the following responses to each card in the lens of Grief and the stages of our processing it as previously discussed.

Should you find your own response differing wildly when you work with any card, then do not hold back from using that. It may be that the deck(s) you work with differ greatly from those that I have used and therefore influence and shape what I derive from them.

What we derive from a card and see in it at a given time may also depend to some extent on what question or subject we have asked for information and guidance on. Do remember to work with the response to the cards you are working with in the light of this. Above all, do not be tempted to just stick to 'what the book says' about your card, whether it is this one, or any other book on Tarot!

When researching the five stages of Grief, both to learn about them for this book, as well as helping my own process, it became apparent that they are presented in predominantly the same order. It is in this order I present them here, this being:

DENIAL   SWORDS

ANGER   WANDS

BARGAINING   PENTACLES

DEPRESSION   CUPS

ACCEPTANCE MAJOR ARCANA

This is not done to suggest that this is the order we either do or should experience or deal with our Grief. As stated before, it is a non-linear and certainly not logical process, and does not fit neatly into boxes such as these. They are however, useful, common traits by which we can help to understand what is going on for us, as we encounter them each time we do.

Where I have made references to the imagery on a card, this is using the Rider Waite Smith deck as the basis, since this is the most widely known deck, along with all its derivatives. What I have written about each card is done so as a reference for you to use as you wish and which I hope serves to help you in dealing with your Grief in a better way.

SWORDS - DENIAL

ACE

The beginning of each of the suits has for me, always represented something new in their particular realm. Here we start with the Mind and the mental level of the human being, and so with this card we have a new state of mind.

With Grief we may be experiencing shock as our initial mental condition, as well as disbelief. This can be particularly so when the death is sudden. That being said, in my own experience even after a lengthy illness, the expected death of my mother still came as a shock.

With all the Swords cards it can be easy to identify them with how we feel, such is the apparent emotional negativity of many of the images. Yet we need to see the Swords as symbols of our mind and what is happening in it. Close to this comes communication, which can be internal and external i.e. with ourselves and others, what we are saying and what we are hearing.

When this card appears it can be helpful to consider what new thoughts are in our mind, those thoughts we would not be having were in not for the death we have experienced in our lives. As an author I am a great believer in writing things down, so a suggestion here is to journal the thoughts you are aware of having. You may ask yourself 'What do I think about this death'? That may seem an obvious thing in some respects but it can be helpful to formulate our thoughts and express them on paper.

We may also want to consider what needs communicating. This can be the mental messages we need to give ourselves as well as anything we may think we need to express to someone else. Ask yourself what do you really want to say that you might feel unable to, or that would not be helpful or even kind to say. It can be helpful to express these on paper, or record yourself. In doing so, do ensure anything you do not want others to see or hear is secure. This is simply a release of mental energy.

The Tarot presents the human being as the four levels of physical, emotional, mental and spiritual, the whole person being the sum greater than these parts. As such for us to be whole and healthy, it is important that each of these levels is balanced with the others. In circumstances such as Grief, it can be all too easy for our mind to become our master. It may be that the energy of this card guides us to remember that our thoughts are not the whole truth. When we have such strength and depth of feeling that grief engenders it can give rise to thinking that is distorted from our usual calmer, more balanced and objective point of view.

There is a direct link between the breath and the mind, and it is true to say that if we want to calm our mind, we need to calm the breath. So in the times and moments where our thoughts are running away with us, or they just turn like a hamster on a wheel in our minds, as surely they are bound to do, we can simply breathe. Taking several full, conscious and deeper breaths can slow and stop that wheel and restore order and common sense to the mind.

Place a hand on your stomach at the level of your navel, and breathe so that your hand moves out on the inhalation. If possible breathe in through the nose and out through the mouth. If you find yourself on the verge of panic, this practice can be very effective.

The energy of this card can be likened to the idea and concept of 'a breath of fresh air'. Taking a walk outside, if possible in a natural setting, even for just a few minutes and breathing consciously for a time, can help shift a dark, limited, oppressive line of thinking to a new one.

TWO

Two is the number for duality, and in the case of our minds, incoming and outgoing thoughts and expression. The standard or common depiction of this card is that of the blindfolded figure on a beach, holding the two Swords over their crossed breast. There is a crescent Moon above, shining its light onto them.

Here the Denial stage may be particularly highlighted. The blindfold can indicate a refusal to see or observe what our reality is – i.e. the death we have experienced. That the Swords are across the chest suggests a protective layer over the heart. Whilst this may be almost a survival instinct when we first experience Grief, it can also be a defense mechanism that tells us we do not want or need to feel any pain. As much as it hurts, and there is arguably no greater or more acute hurt, we do, at some stage, need to open ourselves to it so we do not become limited by or stuck in this phase.

The Moon, as a crescent, is shown in its 'New' phase, and shines its light to the calm sea behind the figure. This can suggest that beneath what may be thoughts of pain, hurt and anguish, there can be calm, which can give rise to a new thing, a new and different reality to be birthed. What matters here is that we allow ourselves, gently and with great compassion, to be open to this, perhaps just a little at a time after the death; just a tiny fraction more each day.

The Swords themselves, if we stick to the idea that they represent thoughts and what is going on in the mind, are held by the figure. For me, this symbolises that they are ultimately under our control. The Denial stage of Grief can be a difficult one to move through, simply because it can be out of control. My experience was that even though I knew and fully acknowledged the reality of my daughter's death, and knew this all too well of course, something in my mind just would not accept it. It was as if it would not go in, like some mathematical equation I could not comprehend. I came to realise because of this that the mental messages I was giving myself were very important to my state of self and well-being.

Rather than trying to counter-act or even ridicule this unreal awareness, I found that telling myself it is OK for these thoughts to be there and that they will pass, when they and my mind, are ready, then I will fully know the reality. This does not happen in one go, where you suddenly become aware it has stopped, but little by little, like the waxing and waning of the Moon.

The duality aspect of the energy of this card can also be about what we are hearing and what we are saying. People can tend to want to help, or give comfort and can give us all kinds of well-meaning advice, suggestions or platitudes. It is not that we are ungrateful for these, but in such times, answers are not what are needed, since there are none. Being heard however, can be huge, so that rather than keeping any thoughts to ourselves, however dark, dreary or dismal they may be, they can be expressed and heard without judgement, appraisal or comment even.

It can also be all too easy for our minds to become somewhat irrational at a time of Grief. It is almost like the opposite end to when we fall in love and everything is a distortion of reality in our romantic bubble. Here the bubble has been fully burst open and we are raw and wounded. This can colour our thinking, itself greatly shaded by our emotions, and so what it can be helpful for us to hear is a calm, objective and rational view of what we are thinking and experiencing at this time.

THREE

This card can be one of the most recognizable in the deck, and it is a very strong image. This is a large red heart, with the three Swords piercing it, with varying degrees of blood-letting depending on the deck. This takes place beneath stormy, dark skies.

When seen, this card tends to create a typical and understandable response of 'that doesn't look good', and it truly doesn't! Yet, with the approach of blending the energy of the number with that of the suit, we have the creativity and productivity of the Three with our thoughts and mental energy. So this card can, or perhaps should, be about using our mind in creative and productive ways.

However, when we are dealing with Grief this can be incredibly hard to do. The oppression we can feel under, the weight that the experience of our loss and sadness can bring, symbolised by those rain-filled clouds, can make even considering being productive in anyway seem like a huge effort. All that we knew that was safe and normal in our life may be gone, and our reality is now a dark one.

Let us again remind ourselves that the Swords represent our thoughts, whether specific ones or lines of thought we seem to be having. We can see that they are sticking into our heart, so whatever it is we are thinking is really not helping us or being productive, other than affirming how bad we feel, how awful life is and that the world is a terribly cruel place. This is not said with any degree of sarcasm at all, since this is precisely what we can be thinking and feeling in the midst of Grief.

As we know, the energy of the Swords cards can be about the Denial stage. Perhaps, when this card appears for us, we may want to consider if we are actually denying ourselves the need to think these awful thoughts. It can be hard to admit that, right now, we hate the world and what has happened, and our beliefs have been rocked. We may need to admit that we feel small, scared and inconsolable. We may actually want, or need, to embrace those feelings and thoughts for a time.

One of the self-help practices I have recommended to my Tarot clients so many times, and which proves itself to be creative and productive, is that of writing down our thoughts. Here, the power can come in knowing that no-one will ever see what we write, and therefore we can and need to be heart-breakingly honest. Write down those thoughts you are having that you know seem to be hurtful, or born of anger, hate, distress or wherever they come from. It may be that you write only a list of words or it may be pages. Simply let your mind have free reign on to the page. This needs to be hand written, not typed then printed, as it is the energy you are letting out that matters here. It does not matter if it is very hard to read.

Give yourself time and keep writing until you feel there is nothing left to say. You may feel somewhat drained at the end but that is a sign you have released this energy. There may of course be emotional release too. After all, pulling Swords out of your heart, even symbolic ones, can be somewhat painful! When you have finished writing, go outside and burn what you have written. You may want to recite a statement along the lines of 'I burn and release all thoughts not productive to my well-being'.

We are not avoiding the dark thoughts we may be having, indeed there may be a very real need to have them. Once admitted and expressed, in a non-harmful but actually creative way, we create space for a different energy in our minds, and we can begin to work on giving ourselves a better mental health.

FOUR

In Grief our minds can be in turmoil. One day, each hour, or even each minute, there can be a whirlwind of myriad thoughts, sometimes a repeating thought that will just not remove itself from our mind. Other days we seem to want to think about anything but the death and loss we have experienced and the person that has died.

Such an output of mental energy can be utterly exhausting. We may take to our bed and fall into some kind of restless sleep, or fitful dozing, only to find when we wake that the dreams we have are equally draining.

The energy of the number four can be like the square, solid, safe and sensible, all things we may not feel or think that we have at this time. The four walls of the square can offer us a boundary, a safe place for our mind to exist in for a time, where it can breathe and relax a little.

This card is often associated with the need for and practice of meditation. Yet in the throes of Grief this may be an impossible thing to achieve - that calm oasis in our minds that typifies the meditative state. I certainly found it very difficult for a time, and this as someone who has meditated regularly for many years. However well-versed in meditation we might or might not be, it can be very hard for our mind to allow ourselves to focus on something other than the variety of aspects associated with Grief.

And yet, the appearance of this card may be suggesting that this is precisely what we need to do, and for that very reason. Our mind may be draining any sense of well-being we might be trying to cling to and be aware of needing.

It may be easier not to consider meditation as a method of emptying the mind, since this is proving to be impossible. A more productive and effective process at this stage may be to simply sit, or lie and allow thoughts to come and go, move through the mind as they will, unchecked, unfiltered and unrestricted. At some point, and there is no right/wrong, better/worse length of time for this, the train of thoughts will begin to slow. If we are patient and remain open, that train will eventually slow to a halt at the station, and maybe even emit some steam just as trains used to do!

This practice does require some persistence and lots of patience. I found I needed to play some suitable music in the background and adopt an attitude of no expectation, measure or concept of any 'success' or effectiveness. Rather I simply did it and stopped when it seemed right. After some time with this I began to feel as if I had been somewhere else for a while, a brief time of respite that gave my mind some kind of holiday. This is not an escape from reality. It is in fact the opposite. It is a means of enabling and empowering your mind to look fully and squarely at the reality you are now faced with.

That said, it can also be helpful to introduce the idea of a 'Sanctuary' you can go to in your mind, to help that idea of giving it a rest and introducing a sense of calm. This may be anywhere you wish, real or imagined, but should not have association with your deceased loved one, for obvious reasons. Such a Sanctuary can have many uses, but for now, it can be seen, in the mind, as a place of temporary refuge and recovery.

FIVE

The standard image of this card can look like the aftermath of a medieval battle, where scavenging of any valuables is done (along with the grisly practice of finishing off the wounded). It is Swords that are the valuables in question here, an interesting concept when we consider them as symbols of our state of mind and thinking. This may suggest that, perhaps contrary to how it might seem, not everything our minds are telling us is negative or nasty. If we care to search amidst the battered remains of the onslaught of Grief in our head, we can find things that may help us.

Much of what I see and term as the therapeutic approach to the Tarot lies in our need to 'face and embrace' the energy of each card, so that we do not become stuck in that place, are able to learn what we need to, and keep moving forward and evolving in our self and life. It is no different with Grief. Though it may feel empty and pointless now, without our loved one to share it, our life still does have meaning, use and purpose, simply because we still exist.

If you feel able to face it, when this card comes out for you, it might be good to consider what you are, have or maybe will one day, learn from all the terrible suffering of Grief. You will know all too well what thoughts you are having that are painful, sad and miserable. Yet, somewhere, squeezed in between those, perhaps tiny and in a barely heard whisper, there may be a thought that says 'I am really going to get on with what I want to do with my life now'.

When my Mother died when I was just 24 years old it came as a shock that I was next as it were – there was no longer a generational barrier between me and death. I resolved then to make the most of my life. I reasoned that I was almost halfway through my life if I used my Mum's age of death as a measure – she was 50 when she died. It was this that ultimately began my career of working with the Tarot and everything associated with it over the years.

Another aspect to this card can be the influence and impact of others thoughts, opinions and communications. The energy of Five can be that of an external influence and here it can take the form of communication. Often people are genuinely sympathetic to us when we are experiencing Grief, and many may have words they think are helpful or comforting. It can be the case though that they do not really touch the pain we feel or the horror of our reality.

Yet, if we stop to consider and listen to at least some of the things said, or written to us, or even those apparently pithy quotes the internet seems swamped with at such times, we may just find something that does resonate with us, that has at least a faint echo of truth in it and that we might memorize and use. We might write it down and place it on the fridge or wherever, and let it become a mantra of healing and positivity rather than wallow in the loss and apparent defeat of our battle.

SIX

I have heard the standard refrain of 'you are moving to calmer waters' so many times with this card over the years that it now makes my toes curl up! It is so said because on one side of the boat that we see being rowed by an often shadowy, guide-like figure the water is choppy, on the other it is calmer. In the boat are two forlorn looking figures, huddled and hooded.

When working our way through the decidedly stormy waters of Grief, if we were to be presented with this image we are far more likely to identify with the figure in the boat rather than the oarsman. The Swords are point down in the boat and would appear to be doing their best to sink it.

For our purposes this suggests that our current way of thinking is not helping us move towards those calmer places. Indeed they may be scuppering our chances of getting there at all. Perhaps it is then that we might benefit from a different view, a more objective one that might tell us a different truth to the one we are currently thinking or experiencing. Perhaps this may come from the shadowy oarsman, whoever they may be.

Six is a number that generally has a benign energy and one that can be of use to us here. In numerological terms, we can see Six as 2 x 3. This suggests the creativity of the three doubled, or given the energy of balance, duality and agreement. We have seen the potentially destructive impact our own thinking may be understandably having at this time. So rather than try to continue with our seemingly futile mental process now, we might consider what it is we need to hear; what do we want to be told. Knowing this is one thing, but actually having it is another. When we are in the midst of Grief our emotions can be just like those choppy waves, effectively giving us thoughts that are very good at sabotaging ourselves.

It can be quite common, and is certainly true in my experience, for us to 'hear' the voice of our deceased loved one, in our minds. This can be especially so in the early days following their passing. This is not necessarily to suggest that they are actually talking to us – I leave that to your own particular beliefs. Either way, their voice may be one of comfort, and even if it is just one of an imagined reality, their perspective might just provide the alternative and more detached view that we need.

Much may depend on your beliefs here, but it is more likely that the majority of people given to working with the Tarot have some kind of belief in an after-life. This being the case we might 'imagine' that the deceased is able to communicate with us and may do so from the vantage point of the 'Spirit world' or whatever term we prefer to use. Given this, they may have a broader perspective than our own. So allowing ourselves this 'fantasy' for this purpose may just give us something that could carry us towards a place where our minds are indeed calmer and more settled.

In addition, and just to mention, there is also the possibility of course that our loved one is actually communicating with us, so if you are open to it, do not dismiss this, but retain a grounded perspective on it.

SEVEN

Here we have a figure who appears to be stealing away with five of the seven Swords in our possession now. He looks to be tip-toeing and his gaze is cast behind him, possibly at the two Swords that remain.

Many Tarot books suggest that Seven is a number that gives us good fortune. When experiencing Grief the suggestion of this is highly likely to be met with a snort of derision, and justifiably so. Seven for me is an energy of the Earth plane and our being upon, or with it. So we can tap into this force by considering our understanding of this, or lack of it, as the case may be.

The Swords being carried away can represent that which we know to be true and perhaps what we have learned from outside sources (there being Five of them). In order to see the two remaining we have to look backwards. This can suggest that, despite all the pain of the Grief, we can still learn from it and there is still a 'plan' for our life, still a purpose for our being here.

When this card appears it may be helpful to consider what the whole experience either has taught or is teaching you. Failing that, we might like to think about what we may eventually learn, once a time has passed.

The scene of this card is unusually pictured at night. This can suggest that it is an inner process in our minds, something private or individual to us. That does not mean we should never discuss these things, but that the learning, and the bigger plan or picture we may need to see now, is ours alone.

Another way we might look at this card is to view the two Swords left behind as representing our loved one and us. This can remind us that, even though they are gone and we are parted, what we had will always remain and be there. We might like to look back and remind ourselves of the beautiful things we shared, in whatever way this was. It can be all too easy in those first days of Grief to mull over the death experience and days/weeks/months leading up to this. That is all natural and may indeed be necessary. Alongside that however, we can also tell ourselves of all the good things we experienced with that person, and what we can take forwards from those things with us, on our own onward journey.

It can be a comfort, as well as therapeutic for ourselves, to list what we have learnt from our deceased loved one, that we can apply to our own life. We may share with someone, whether that person knew them or not, the good memories we have of times together. Whilst this may be emotional, it can be cathartic, as well as a reminder of lovely things. This may unearth forgotten aspects of that person or scenarios where we might apply learning in ourselves and lives, now and onwards.

EIGHT

Here the image is one that when dealing with Grief we would all too readily identify with. It shows a blind-folded figure on the shore, bound by cords, exposed to the Elements and surrounded on most sides by Swords, almost as tall as them, stuck into the ground. The image is a desolate, lonely one that can serve as an adequate description of many people's mental state when going through Grief.

There can be a strong sense that no-one can really know what it's like for us, even those who can truly empathise from having been in a similar situation. They may not have known the person who has died and even if they did, their relationship with them was different to ours. Each person has their own relationship with any other person and so the experience of Grief can be equally individual. We can certainly be left with an awareness in our minds that no-one knows what it is like for us.

There can also be an incredibly frustrating inability to find words that sufficiently express what we are feeling and experiencing. The phrase 'there are no words' can effectively be used, but there is something within us that wants to find words, so that we can be heard and understood for what we are going through. In itself this can bring comfort and some kind of healing.

The appearance of this card may be suggesting that we need to try and find words, however weak they might initially feel, and use whatever words at our disposal. As an author, I love words and Amy tells me I have so many of them! And yet, there is no word in my personal dictionary, or thesaurus, that serves as equal to my experience of the death of my daughter. Expressing those I do have however, is certainly helpful, if for nothing else than helping to release the pent-up, bound, mental energy we see depicted here.

It may depend on your character, but useful practices here can be to ask a friend to be with you while you talk. They do not have to say or do anything, other than the occasional nod or yes to let you know someone is listening. They certainly do not have to provide answers, or offer insights, other than that they understand what you are saying. It is irrelevant whether they agree with you or not. They just need to hear you, while you talk at them. In this context and scenario, everything you say is ok.

If you are someone who finds such openness of mind and heart difficult – and this is no better or worse than if you do not – then you might like to take up the offer a friend of mine made for me. This was of him driving me somewhere so that I could 'scream some fucks at the Universe'! It can really be quite a powerful mental, as well as emotional release to do this. At the shore, as shown in this card, is a perfect place to do so, at night if you are self-conscious! Your choice of vocabulary is yours alone, but if no word strikes you as appropriate, then a simple scream, yell or 'barbaric yawp' as the great Walt Whitman termed it, will suffice more than perfectly well. Verse 52 of his poem 'Songs of Myself', from which this comes, is worth reading with regard to Grief and could almost have been written about this card.

The experience of this card can be when we just cannot talk about our sense of loss and everything else that comes with it. Its appearance can be a reminder that, in whatever way, so long as it does not harm another, it needs a release at some stage or we remain its prisoner.

NINE

It is perhaps not surprising, given the nature of many of the images typical in this suit, that we begin our journey through the Tarot with it and that it is identified with the Denial stage of the Grief process. Taking the images at face value, they can seem to depict our not wanting or being unable to face the reality and the truth behind our Grief and simply not knowing what to say or how to respond to the death of our loved one.

A casual glance at this image confirms all the above. It typically shows someone sitting up in bed at night, their head in their hands, the nine Swords arranged above them, symbolic of their mind that will just not switch off and let them sleep.

Sleep can become an all too rare and precious commodity in the throes of Grief, especially so in the first days of course. In itself this can be draining, and result in a lack of ability to focus mentally, or 'think straight' as the saying goes'. Thinking straight implies logical thought and this may not be possible at such a time. It may help not to try to do so, to avoid further frustration and confusion, such is the mental energy with this card. We can permit ourselves to go from one random thought or another, knowing that somewhere in them there is one that is right. Our gut will tell us what this is and when we have it. This can be with regard to what we need, from minute to minute if necessary.

Perhaps it is that you need some air – step outside and breathe, even if it is 3 am. Maybe you need to drink some water, then do so. Do you need to cry, and look at a photo of your loved one? Do that, even if you are in the supermarket. You don't need to bawl loudly, but shedding some tears is a perfectly natural thing. Stand by the onions and blame it on them if need be! Addressing your own needs in this way can help release what is nearly always an over-burdened, over-active mind when this card comes out.

Nine is a number of highest activity and productivity (as 3 x 3) and this very often manifests in disturbed sleep. This can be not being able to get to sleep, or doing so – swiftly and easily because we are exhausted - only to wake up again, and be wide-awake at various intervals. It can be useful to have a notebook and pen, or voice recorder, next to us and to put whatever we have in our mind there when we wake. It does not matter what these are, whether they make sense or if they are related in any way to our Grief. It is simply about releasing some of the excess of mental energy.

Many dreams can be the result of thoughts in our mind that are unprocessed when we go to sleep. The deeper layers of our mind can get to work, to deal with whatever is floating about. The experience of Grief can therefore give rise to many dreams, which may feel significant. When we wake, allowing ourselves to just lie there and consider our dream can help to recall it, and then to write it down/record it. It is not necessarily required to analyse or interpret the dream, but it can be another release of mental excess that of itself is entirely therapeutic and productive.

TEN

We come now to the last numerical card of this suit, where looking at this image, it seems that the mind has won the battle. It shows all ten Swords sticking in the back of their victim, who lies on the shore at night, bleeding beneath the dark clouds of gloom above. Again, something else we can readily identify with, in Grief.

As I do frequently in my readings with clients, let us remind ourselves again that the Swords are symbols of our thoughts and our mental activity. So what here, has died? Of course we know our loved one has, but we are looking at ourselves now and how we can respond to our Grief in response to this.

It can be a common practice for us to quantify our lives and its stages by the different significant occurrences over the years. This may be such things as completing education, beginning our career, getting married, having our first child, the death of a parent, the birth of a grandchild and so on. It is easy to see such things as birth and death experiences, whether symbolic or literal.

In writing this book my aim is that it helps those who are dealing with Grief, and the assumption is that if you are reading it, the death has had a strong enough impact upon you to qualify as one significant enough to be added to the list above, of your own life. A look at this card and seeing what reaction you have will soon confirm if this is the case.

We cannot argue with death, we cannot stop it or pretend it will not happen. It is this that I see as the victory in this card, and also its therapy. As the last card of the suit, the Ten can be about letting go, releasing, getting rid and divesting ourselves of all that we have been holding on. Mentally this can be a sense of being completely drained, empty of mind, knowing and understanding. In the case of my daughter, there seemed to simply be no reason at all why she should die in such a way as she did and at such an age. It was a case of trying to get to a point in my mind where I had to come to know it simply was and is, and without any reason or logic.

The more we look for an explanation or an answer to this, even some or any kind of understanding, the more tortuous and harmful to the self it can become. The victory can come in the admittance that we do not have an explanation, that there is none, there is no sense in it, there was nothing we could ultimately do about it; the death has happened and it cannot be changed.

This does not mean of course that we have 'got over it' or even at this stage fully accepted it; only that we admit we don't know anything at all about it, other than that it has happened. It is bigger and stronger than us and so we give up trying to rationalize it, trying to work it out and understand it. It simply is. And so the death here is to that part of us in our mind that wants to 'know', that seeks to give comfort and solace by being able to explain it. When we can come to a realisation that the only way we can do this is to know we cannot explain the unexplainable, then our minds can begin to become free of the swords in our back.

PAGE

In keeping with my therapeutic approach to the Tarot, my stance with the Court cards is to work with what I see as their energy. This may be expressed through a personality in our life, whether our own or someone else's. More particularly in terms of Grief, they can typify character traits or approaches we may find helpful to adopt at a particular time or in a specific situation we find ourselves in.

Just as with the number cards the basic energetic make-up of the card can come from combining the suit with the number, here we combine the suit with the element the cards belongs to. In the case of the Pages, this is Earth, and its associated qualities, as given in the tables in Chapter 1. So for the Pages of Swords we combine Air and Earth, the Mind and the Body.

So the central core of the Swords Page (put this way to remind us that the energy of the suit comes first) is that of thinking before we act, planning what we might do, and to avoid rushing in to things without a pause to at least consider options.

When we are raw and bruised in our Grief, it can be tempting to want to cling to the first thing that is available to us. It can be very easy to act without thinking, since we may want to reach for anything that will lesson our pain and bring some comfort. This could take all manner of forms, and some of course, may be wiser than others.

Whilst I have earlier advocated the practice of addressing your needs from one minute to the next, the guidance was to think about what they are. Here the Page may be counselling us to do this. Before we embark on a course of action, stop and think. This might be something small, or the beginning of a longer term plan we want to put into practice, now that our loved one has gone.

The Page is learning to consider the implications and ramifications of what he is thinking about. He may be somewhat slow to act, but here the energy suggests that this is preferable to acting without thinking. As we know, Swords connect us with communication, so it can be sensible to discuss our plans with someone before we swing into action.

Equally, he does have an impulse to do something. So this card may be telling us that once we are clear and have made our decision, the need is indeed to act. It simply needs to be done in tandem, or balance, with what our minds are suggesting, and give this adequate consideration first. The 'success' or best response to the Court cards invariably comes from a measured and balanced response to the twin energies they each have.

The atypical response the Swords Page has to a situation, is first 'what do I think about this', followed by 'what do I need to do about it'.

KNIGHT

Following our elemental approach to the Court cards, here we have the combination of Air with Fire. The image of our bold Knight certainly suggests we have someone who is fired up, yet he is fueled by a certainty of mind, typified by a fixed stare directly ahead. The motivation and fuel here comes from being clear of mind, a fixed intent and clear purpose in his head and perhaps a target he is aiming for.

With regard to Grief such clarity of mind as we have seen on our path through this suit, can be all too hard to find. Indeed, we may not even know if it is day or night, or what day it is when the dawn eventually comes, let alone what we can do about getting motivated to achieve anything.

And yet, however bad we might be at any one given time, we still have a fire within us. This might be in the form of what it is that makes our heart beat, our blood to be warm and what makes it continue to flow through us. We have a life-force within us that cannot be switched off like a light. It remains a resource within us, however dim and tiny it may become, that we can turn to and use whenever we have need.

For the Swords Knight, this begins in the mind and perhaps by asking 'what is fueling me'? It can be the simple question of 'why' when we are considering what to do with our lives now that our loved one is no longer part of it Everything may have changed as a result of their death and we can be aimless, everything seem to lack meaning and purpose.

So it is we may need to find a new one, and Swords Knight suggests we ask ourselves about this and identify what our motive is in life now; where is it coming from and what is its purpose? We read many times of those who are spurred into a course of action following the death of a loved one to do something with themselves and their life they may never have considered otherwise.

This does not suggest we all have to or should embark on some fund-raising epic, admirable though these may be. Rather Swords Knight may be telling us to think about what we have done with our lives thus far and what we are motivated or driven to do now, in the light of the loss of our loved one.

Equally, he can also suggest that once we tap into this fuel, the need can be to respond to it; to feel the fire and use that inner resource to go after our goal. I am reminded here of the quote, attributed to the 'German Shakespeare' Goethe: 'Whatever you can do or dream you can begin it. Boldness has genius or magic in it'. This can be the Swords Knight's gift to you.

QUEEN

The Queens are traditionally related to the element of Water and therefore its associations with feelings and the emotions. This is blended here with Air, the head, and thinking.

I mentioned previously that the Court cards require a balance of their two energies to be used and responded to if we are to heed or respond well to their counsel. This card – along with its 'polar opposite', (King of Cups) relate to a combination of head and heart. As such it could be argued that this can be a tricky combination to achieve. Equally, when this is achieved, it provides for a sense we can justifiably call 'knowing' or a surety of self, since it comes from both what we think and what we feel rather than (predominantly) one or the other.

Being of Swords the Queen here will always consider first what she thinks about what she encounters. Her initial reaction to life and what it present here is to think. This gives rise to her feelings and desire. Put another way, she needs to be able to understand something if she is able to connect any sense of emotion to a thing, person or situation. In another sense, for her to love someone, she has to be able to first communicate with them.

The appearance of the Swords Queen can be asking you to think about the state of your own heart too. Of course when we are experiencing Grief our emotions can be intense, and we may be prone to more extreme lows, as well as highs. Our sensitivity to emotional stimulus may be heightened and this can easily create a distortion in our awareness and perceptions. The Queen may be reminding us of the need to keep a clearer view and a more balanced way about us right now.

This is not to dismiss our feelings, far from it. Her guidance is simply that we need to think first, as all the Swords courts suggest. Once we have engaged our brain, with regard to whatever may be happening to us when this card appears, then we can tap into how we feel about it.

It can be that in the throes of our Grief either the head or the heart claims dominance over us, very often without our being aware of it. We are each pre-disposed to be led by the head or the heart, what we think or what we feel. Neither is better or worse, but we do tend to gravitate to one or the other. When under the stress and duress of Grief we can turn to this as something to rely on and where we feel safe. You will know within whether your natural tendency is to go to your head or heart.

It is by taking both head and heart into account that we can arrive at that deeper level of knowing however. Something that can be useful to help us arrive at this balance is to draw a straight line down the middle of a sheet of paper, and head one half Heart, the other Head. Beneath each we can then list the main or strongest thoughts/feelings we are having. The length of each list can tell us much by itself, but we can also see how one list relates to the other. This can be seeing what thoughts give rise to particular feelings and so on. I have found this to be a useful method of raising some objectivity and increasing my awareness of self.

KING

There is one card in each suit that has double the strength of one Element, in this case of course that being Air. We know that Swords relate to Air, and so too do the Kings. The result of this combination can of course make our lofty King here something of an 'air-head', someone who can be very clever, objective, analytical and intelligent, yet lack common-sense, compassion and practicality. He can be the archetypal 'mad professor'.

What then can he have to teach us in our Grief? It may seem desirable to want to 'take a step back' and look at things objectively and with a level head, but that can be virtually impossible when the weight of our feelings is so heavy that we are lodged firmly in the tears of our heart. Yet, a more detached place can be helpful, even if only for a brief space of time.

The King may be able to help us with this. We can consider 'what would the Swords King do' when faced with our dilemma, or whatever it is we are facing when he comes out of the deck to greet us. A way to access this in a measured, as well as fun way, is to have a conversation with him. As before, we can write this, or perhaps record it. If you know someone who knows the Tarot well, they could play the part of the King for you.

You might begin with telling him about your situation, or how you feel, or anything that you wish to say or share. Without pausing, allow yourself to respond from the Kings position, that of someone who is 'in their head' and applying their mental energy entirely to this situation. Letting your responses be immediate is a way for your intuition to guide you, through the lens of the King.

An additional aspect for the Swords King can be a complete lack of practicality. He may be able to write a brilliant thesis, but if asked to carry out a practical task his analysis of everything before he did it would take an eternity! He has an ongoing need to ground himself and keep his feet on the earth. We may have a need to consider how grounded we are when he appears and whether we need to get in touch with what needs doing. It can be easy to make grand plans when such a big life-shift as a loved one dying has happened, but acting on them is a different thing.

Whilst he may lack the sensitivity of his Queen, his appearance does not need to suggest that we need to bottle our emotions up or suppress them, Part of his wisdom is that he can remind us that our feelings will pass. How things are in this moment may not be as they are in the next. What may appear black as coal one day may seem brighter the next. The King can be helpful in reminding us of cold truths that, on occasions, we do need to hear.

WANDS - ANGER

ACE

If we look at the five stages of Grief as a continuous process, regardless of the fact that we do not experience them that way, we can see a progression from where we were at in the Ten of Swords to this card. It can help to quantify the Grief process and the Tarot for ourselves by moving from one suit to the next in this way.

With the Ten of Swords we found ourselves somewhat confronted with the stark facts of the death of our loved one but unable to 'get our heads around it', and this inability resulting in damage to the self in terms of our mental state, a disbelief, a state of unreality, perhaps self-blame and an absence of reason.

I mentioned in that card that the death of our loved one is something that 'just is'. This is also the case with this card, but at a more energetic or perhaps fundamental level in our make-up, attitude and self generally. It is as if the Universe is presenting us with this unasked for event and saying 'what will you do with that'. We have this experience, whether for the first time in our life or another time, but each time we have to draw in and come to terms with the energy of this.

This can mean in terms of our inner self, our character; the impact of the death experience on us as a person. It is a force that we experience, or are given, if we see it that way, and we have to respond one way or another. In order to work out what that response needs to be, we first need to know what this force is and what our instinctive response is. This is the experience and need with this card.

This can be a very raw thing, as if it peels our skin back and bares our very essence. It can be very hard to give the energy of this card terms and labels, but that can be a useful thing to do, simply to help us be aware of it, rather than trying to be logical about it. It is anything but and its very nature can result in that sense within us of 'not knowing what to do about it'.

The simple response to this is that we do not need to know. It can be enough for it to simply be there, something within us that requires first our recognition and then a response. It reminds me of the 'primal scream' of Arthur Janov in the 1970's.

Just as the Aces of each suit contain the pure, raw essence of their elemental energy, here we have the nature of Fire. One thing we do know of Fire is that if left unattended it can cause untold destruction and damage. We therefore need to do something with this energy, this force within us.

In terms of the stages of Grief, we arrive at Anger now. It is easy to think of Anger as a negative thing and something to be avoided, especially if we are 'spiritual'! Regardless of how spiritual we may think we are, we are still a human being and we can still be angry - we are allowed! Rather than allow our anger to remain unchecked and become destructive, we can choose to give ourselves an outlet; to release the energy as an expression of what we feel.

What we do for this may depend on the type of person you are. I find that going for a run or some vigorous exercise helps shift it, sometimes by shouting or screaming into the wind as I go. Standing on top of a hill and yelling for all your worth is an exhilarating, as well as effective response here. You might prefer to hit a cushion or pillow (do air or wash it afterwards to clear the anger energy). I saw a TV piece about a place in the US where old cars and machines are kept for people to go and smash them, just for this purpose! Whatever you do, it is about sensing what this anger is within you and how you need to express it.

TWO

Whilst the numerical energy of Two is seen as balance and duality, this can sometimes have the effect of balancing things out to an extent where there is no active dynamic at all, and everything stays the same. We can 'carry on regardless' following our Grief experience, or it could serve as something of a catalyst that does indeed, galvanize us into action.

When I experienced my Mother's death at her relatively young age of 50, with my being 24 at the time, one of the major responses I had was that of it galvanizing me into action in my own life. After a time and the reality had kicked in, there was a mental realisation that there was no longer that generational gap between myself and death. There is a certain psychological barrier between the prospect and reality of your own death whilst you have a parent alive. Once they have gone, you are next!

This led me to realise that life is, or can be, short. Either way it goes quickly and there is no point in wasting time and energy in not doing what we really want. At the time I had a mortgage and a 'good', steady job. Yet this was not what I really wanted to do. Within the space of a couple of years my life changed dramatically. I no longer worked full-time, and had begun my work with Tarot which has since shaped the last 35 years and become my 'career'.

The energy of this card seems to sum up that response. It can be about how we handle the frustration we might feel following a loved ones' death, as we look at our own new situation. There may be anger too of course, but beneath this there can often be this sense from within that life is not as we would wish it to be. That may well be because our loved one has died and left a massive hole in it. Our need is then to peer into that hole and decide what we would fill it with.

We might like to ask ourselves those somewhat clichéd but still applicable and useful questions – 'If not you, who'? and 'If not now, when'? In the context of our Grief this can be about what we will do now that our loved one is no longer part of our lives. If we are feeling the Anger of this stage of Grief, the energy of this card can be calling us to consider what we will do with that Anger. Will we allow it to frustrate us and see the world only as something of an enemy and a cruel place to navigate, or will we use that force to spur us forwards and onwards, even if we do not know how, when or where just yet?

It may be that we have a sense of not wanting to go on after our loved one's death. We may feel as if our life force has cancelled itself out and our motivation has sunk so low. Life without them just will not be the same. Nor will it of course, and yet we cannot completely rub out the energy of the life-force within us. We still wake up after whatever sleep we are able to get because of it and at some point, we will feel hunger. These are basic survival traits our life-force gives us.

The energy of this card comes down to how we will respond to that inner energy we still have now. What will we do with it and how will we use it? Ultimately the main thing at this stage may be simply to avoid doing nothing.

THREE

The Three of Wands is a card that can be easily seen as a 'past, present, future' energy, with one of the wands representing one each of these. We can also apply this to our Grief process. We can have a tendency to look at our life in stages, marked by the major events and happenings we experienced as we went. The death of those significant to us can be one or more of those stages.

Where we are dealing with the aftermath of the death of a loved one, we can see our self in the context of how things were before their death and how they are after it. The 'in-between' stage is where we are at now - the process of our Grief and how we react and respond to it.

It is often said that we should 'respond, not react'. Yet with Anger this can be a difficult thing to do, not least in the case of an anger, sense of injustice or pointlessness we have at this death. We should not pretend we are not feeling these things if we are. Indeed it can be an entirely necessary thing to acknowledge the energy we have. It is this that can shift us from reacting – in the sense of without any regard or care for anything else – to a more considered and conscious response.

Looking at the content of the 'before, during and after' of our Grief process can be a helpful response to this card. When we are caught up in the energy of anger, frustration and all that can come with or be part of these things, a process that enables us to step outside of what can be an all too encompassing state, it can prove a vital turning point, helping us deal with where we are at, and move forwards.

The energy of the Three can give us this inner need, where we may not know where our lives and self could now be headed. The road ahead may be one long blind curve, assuming we can see a road at all at this point. And yet we do sense there is, or has to be, some kind of future ahead of us. It may be that we cannot sense anything other than something stretching out before us that only amplifies the loss we have had.

Our need here may be to put this into a context beyond this blinkered, tunnel-vision view. We can try the practice of listing the things that were important to us in our life before the death occurred. Next we can list what seems important to us now. We can then see ourselves in the place between these things. We can look at what the 'future' list has that the 'past' list does not. By asking ourselves what is required to create, or begin to take a step towards one of those things, we can begin to formulate a plan of action, something at least to aim for, even if we just cannot manage to actually do anything about it just yet.

This card has always seemed to me to naturally follow on from the Two of Wands, similar as it is in its traditional design, colouring and symbolism. The exercise above enables us to tap into that potential force within us with the Two and give it some sense of purpose, direction and perhaps even meaning, with the Three.

FOUR

The experience of the death of a loved one is always something of a shock. This can be the case even if the death has been a gradual or protracted process and we have been doing what we can to prepare ourselves. When it does happen, the shock can still be there. In the case of a sudden, violent, accidental or totally unexpected death, that shock can be magnified, to a seemingly insurmountable level.

My Mother was diagnosed with the cancer that killed her and was given a year or so to live. She lived for three however. When the call came the night she died, as I knew earlier that evening that it would, it was still a shock. I went quiet and was asked if it was a shock. Given the situation, I said that oddly, it was. There is a big difference between an expectation and a reality, especially when it is something you do not want to be so.

We can be jolted out of our place of known comfort and security. There we are one day, living our lives, bumbling along as best we can with nothing too dramatic to rock the boat or threaten our well-being. Then along comes the death of someone we love, and it is as if our boat has sprung a leak, as if all that we knew for sure and was safe and comforting in our lives has gone.

Our instinct and reaction to this can be to immediately grasp to get back what was lost, to reclaim that security and familiarity and find something that brings us comfort, and tells us that everything is, or will be, ok. This is the energy of this card, and in a time of Grief, it can be completely understandable. A routine of what is known to us may be precisely what we need to help us navigate those first terribly painful, lonely days and weeks.

Everything will indeed be ok, but it will not be the same. The appearance of this card may be nudging you towards a need to recognise this, even as your need and instinct may be for the comfort and security of the familiar. This is all amplified in situations where we lived with the loved one who has died.

Trying to maintain a status quo in our lives, in whatever way, can be a futile thing, since something has shifted within us. Our motives for our life and how we live it may need to change. The energy of this card may be calling you to look within to this part of yourself before you look without and take action. The counsel of this card may be to stop and take stock, rather than rushing ahead. Allow yourself to get comfortable with the idea of the new, and when you sense you are on a more stable platform, then you can begin to move towards that next stage.

As can be common with the Tarot, and arguably in particular with the suit of Wands, the need this card may be highlighting is that of looking at our self and life objectively. We can see the cards as if we are the actor in the play of our life, as indeed may be what was intended by Pamela Colman-Smith of the ubiquitous Rider-Waite-Smith Tarot. Look out from our vantage point on the stage - what are we projecting and what do we wish to create?

The security that the energy of this card highlights is, in Grief, no longer what it was. Instead, a new one needs to be found and established, and this can take some force of will, followed by expression of that will before it can begin to become established in both our self and our life. This card may help to begin that process.

FIVE

The aftermath of a death of a loved one can leave us all over the place and in a state of 'not knowing which way is up', or certainly what day it is. The initial few days, maybe even weeks or months, can be fraught with nights blurring into days as we nod off now and again, only to wake with the thoughts and mental imprint of what has happened raging through our minds. The cycle of day following night can become indistinct and we simply exist, moving from one bit to the next.

If we eat much for a while it is all too often something we can simply pick up and eat, or these days have delivered to our home. The thought of cooking a meal as we might usually do is just too much, let alone the idea of sitting down to eat a full meal. We are, as perhaps we just need to be for a time, all over the place. Routine is something that goes, along with our loved one's passing.

This is how we can see what is usually depicted in this card, that of the different aspects of the self all vying for attention and trying to get in control, be acknowledged and heard. The result of all this tumult is confusion, exasperation, anger certainly, and often a degree of what may best be described as chaos.

What may be needed when this card appears for us is again something that will help us regain some semblance of 'normality' or a small sense of order and structure where there is none. Rather than trying to identify which parts of ourselves are most in need or most deserve to be heard, we can allow each its voice and chance to speak.

We could do this by listing on paper the different things that are occupying us at this time – the thoughts we are having, the feelings that we have, the things we want to do, or not do, or feel we ought to do but are not, the responses we think we should be having, and may or may not be. There can be something of a pressure to behave or be a certain way when we are grieving, but that may not suit us, or it may simply not fit with our character, or be what we feel like doing at this point. There are no rules. Once we have our list we can prioritise from it by deciding from what jumps out at us as the most appealing thing to focus on first.

It may be that in our state of 'not knowing' as described above, we need to try one thing and see if indeed it is what we need. If it is not, stop it and start doing a different thing. Perhaps it is that we need to do nothing and this in itself becomes the 'thing' that we need. Only by doing so and giving ourselves the permission and acknowledgment of our need can we be ok with it.

There can also be many demands made upon us, either by ourselves and the energies within us, or by others and the demands of the world at such a time. This may depend on your status with regard to the loved one. In such situations the need can be strongly for objectivity and planning. Perhaps with the help of someone who is slightly more removed from the situation than us, we can be greatly helped by simply listing what needs doing, and take one at a time, rather than our energy and focus being scattered, and a sense of chaos engulfing us.

SIX

Traditionally, this card is seen as indicating triumph, the victory parade having vanquished our enemies. When we are in Grief there is of course a total absence of anything like this. Victory and winning may be the very last things we are concerned with and an understandable response to this suggestion would be that there is the opposite, a loss - of both our loved ones life and their absence in our life.

Someone said to my wife after our daughter's death 'just think, in a couple of years or so you'll have got over all this and won't feel like this anymore'. Much as this was intended to be an encouragement, the idea of getting over such a loss did not and does not enter the equation at all, and nor should it. Instead, the aim can be to reach a stage of acceptance, of learning from the experience and applying that learning in some way, even growing from it. This could be seen as a victory, of some sort.

While we are in Grief, and again especially so in its initial throes, it can be hard to find any motivation, to do pretty much anything some days and generally for the things we usually do in our day. The will is just not there. We may be able to force ourselves to do some things, others we might not, even though we know we should. We fail, we do not succeed, and that is understandable and acceptable.

What we can do is look back at each day and see what we may have succeeded at however. This may be only that we made ourselves a hot drink, where before we couldn't be bothered. Did we heat some food, stretch our body at some stage, take a wash or shower, speak with someone, even speak with someone about something other than death, loss, the deceased and Grief? Write these things down, and add to them each day.

Doing this enables us to realise that no matter how much we feel like it, we are not a total failure; there have always been some victories, triumph over this considerable adversity we are facing. This also creates a powerful and comforting tool. In our darkest moments when it may all seem just too much to bear and deal with, we can grab this list and see and remind ourselves that we did succeed at something, even just one thing, and knowing this, we can repeat it.

That one victory can lead to another and that inner force of motivation and will gets fed. This is the fire inside. It may not be experienced as Anger but it is clear that in this suit we see anger partly as a motivational force that can be put to good use in this light, of Grief.

Another aspect that may be worth exploring when this card appears for you is to consider the achievements, and victories, the deceased had in their life. It can be all too easy to look at the loss and sadness that comes with a death and this is necessary of course. Yet it is good and motivating for those of us still here to fully and properly remind ourselves of all that the deceased did in their life. This is not done from a nostalgic perspective, though this can bring comfort too, but of actually coming to realise the good that they did and use this as part of our future motivation.

When my 'best friend' died, at her funeral there was a recount of her life such as this, and it really made clear all that she had done. I had been asked to speak, and following this tale of her life, I began by saying "What a woman"! We can use this energy to help ensure we leave behind our own triumphs and victories for others to learn and grow from.

SEVEN

It is possible to see this card as representing either attack or defence. It usually shows a figure who is either defending his positon from an attack of wand-bearing foes, or seen a different way, a person who is putting his best foot forward and attacking what is in his way. Either way, the image can highlight the basic force and energy of anger that we may well be experiencing when this card comes to us.

Anger is a perfectly understandable thing to experience following the death of someone we love. What seems to matter more is what we do with that energy; how we respond to it. We may be tempted to lash out in our anger, spitting our fury at any who dare to try and come close to us, or to the world and its ways in general. If you have this kind of anger, a suggestion may be to seek an outlet that is not harmful or destructive to another living being. As mentioned before, beating up a cushion, or smashing appropriate objects can be wonderfully therapeutic.

It can be helpful to identify the object(s) of our anger – what or who are we feeling a desire to direct our anger at? Once we have realised these things we may be more able to find a productive or better outlet for this energy. We may benefit from considering how our view of the world and our life has changed as a result of the death we have experienced.

It may be that we do not have a focus for our anger, we simply are angry, at the fact that the death has happened and our inability to stop it or do anything about it. Once we get to a place in ourselves of knowing this, we may be able to find appropriate expression for our anger which in turn may allow us to rationalize and understand it more. In these ways we may be able to turn what seems a destructive force into a productive one.

One way or another, we need to release the anger from within us, and to do so in such a way that does not inflict harm on another. Should we bottle this up or suppress it, it can result in a hardness and bitterness, a defence mechanism that no-one can break through and that also results in our being unable to feel love fully again, or experience pleasure in its fullest and deepest sense.

There is an adage that says 'attack is the best form of defence'. In the context of dealing with Grief, we may well feel in need of defence, from our pain, from the raw wound we have suffered, from the cruelty of the world, even the good intentions of others around us. Before we go into attack mode however, we may want to consider what it is we want to attack and why this is so. What force is causing us to do this and what is the best, productive method of bringing this about?

It can also be that our usual sense of proportion, reason and balance at this time is somewhat compromised. When we are processing our Grief it is easy to think we are seeing things clearly when in fact everything is distorted by the force within us resulting from the pain we have. The appearance of this card may be suggesting to us that we need to come to an understanding of our basis state of self at this time and give ourselves some tender care, love and compassion.

EIGHT

We each respond differently to Grief. We know that we can classify our experiences into the five stages we have here, but how we do this, in what manner and through what specifics, is particular to each of us. There is no right or wrong.

Some people want to respond immediately to the death, and get everything done that needs doing, which depending on our position in relation to the deceased person, can be much. We may rush around, doing part of one thing, then something else and so on. The danger here is that we can exhaust our already depleted energy until eventually we collapse in a heap, unable to do anything or be of any use whatsoever.

The appearance of this card can manifest that kind of energy, creating an almost false kind of urgency where there actually is none. Again, in its wider sense in this suit, the energy of Anger is a force within us looking for an outlet that can show itself in this type of need to get things done. An attempt to create some order out of the ensuing chaos following a death can be useful but may need to happen in a more measured and controlled way than our inner urge might be pushing us to. It can be good to be mindful of trying to force any outcomes now.

Of course it may be that we go the other way and this active energy within may be exactly what we need. We may find, as a general state of being or just on any one day that we just cannot find the motivation or the will to get going.

In such cases, either over or inactivity is fine and understandable and we do need to avoid feeling bad about being this way. It is simply how we are, and we are allowed to be like it.

In regard to how we find a motivation when it is lacking, an objective view can be helpful. This can begin with knowing we are like this and reminding ourselves that it is indeed ok. We can then look realistically at what our options are in light of this. We can stay in bed all day, or turn the TV on and vegetate. Some might get drunk, others might literally sit and stare at the wall. Some may be less advisable than others, but all are options.

Another option might be to make ourselves do one thing, however small. Forcing an action, such as standing up and walking into the kitchen, means there is a movement of energy where there was none before. We can then convert that into another force, and then action. This might be making a cup of coffee, then calling or at least texting someone, and so on.

I sometimes use an analogy from my own experience to illustrate this. I am one of those people who loves to go out running now and again. Once I am out there, I can go where I like. It is the one time I cannot be contacted and I can be free of any concerns, other than breathing and keeping going. The key part here is 'once I am out there'. It is said that the hardest step is running is the first one out the door. Once you have started you just keep putting one foot in front of the other and then just keep doing it. It is determining beforehand to do so where the struggle takes place.

I have learnt over the years, with regard to running and other exercise I do too, as well as many situations in my life that occur, that making myself begin or start doing something when I know I don't really want to makes it easier, and that the hardest part is already done.

NINE

This is one of the cards where I have always felt that the traditional image does not fit with the formula of numerical energy plus suit type. There is usually an image of a bandaged, battered and bruised person, leaning on a wand looking as if he will collapse if he does not have it to hold him up. The remaining eight wands are arranged in a line behind him.

It may well be that this is an image you can identify fully with, whilst dealing with your Grief. The wands behind can be representative of all that we have been through, as well as those around us and of course our loved one who has died. The wands are usually taller than the figure here and this seems in keeping with how things can seem and what we have experienced – they are bigger and stronger than us.

Now that we have been 'dragged through the hedge backwards' as the saying goes, here we are, clinging on to what we have left. So what is that something? It can be good to identify this – what and/or who is our support now, what is sustaining us in these days and nights of agony and loss? The fact is we are still here and something is keeping us going, even if that is just sheer bloody-mindedness, will power, or indeed anger. It is a force and energy we can tap into and turn into what we need next.

It may help to list what is sustaining us at this time down one side of a page, and next to each thing – however short or long our list might be – we can write our response to it - what it is we can do with that, to use it to help keep us going and improve out lot. We then have a plan of actions we can take to move forwards with.

If we do look at this card in terms of combining the numerical energy of the Nine with the fire of the suit, we arrive at a different scenario. Nine is of course the highest single digit and as such can represent the pinnacle, the highest achievement and object of what we are aiming for, a realisation of our goals, and a belief that we can achieve anything. Numerology tells us that three is the power of creativity, so here, multiplied by itself, it becomes the result of that.

What strikes as the most meaningful for us as we deal with Grief from this interpretation, is the strength of the inner belief and will-power. This may be very low as we process our Grief, so knowing somewhere in our being, however buried this may seem at present, lies the surety that we can succeed can be such a strength. We can get to a place where the sadness, loss and despair is not all consuming and there is once again love, joy and purpose in our life and the world.

Looked at in this way, we can welcome the appearance of this card as a promise for a future, if not our present. It can act as a reminder for us that we are not beaten yet and that we have resources deep within the well of our being, hidden at present maybe, submerged beneath tides of emotions that weigh us down right now, but there, all the same. Something still maintains us, and here we have a reminder that this is something that needs no analysis, explanation or even understanding. It is simply there, it is part of us and it *will* serve us as we need.

TEN

When someone close to us dies, there is a great deal to do. Depending on our position there can be all the practicalities to deal with, the funeral - which is way more than the service/ceremony itself – dealing with legalities, any property, possessions, informing people and so on. We may find ourselves shouldering responsibilities for many things we would really rather not do, each one becoming another burden we feel we need to carry.

This can all become too much and we can feel like we are carrying everything, when all we want to do is 'sit upon the ground and tell sad stories of the death of Kings' (Shakespeare's Richard 11: Act 3, Scene 2). It may be that this is indeed the counsel of this card. Consider whether you are shouldering too much, or perhaps filling your days, and perhaps nights, with tasks, finding 'things' that need doing and sorting out, thereby avoiding the very thing that you need to do.

If this is you, you can be sure that the exhaustion you feel as a result is not only because of all that you have and may be still doing, but also because you are carrying an energy that needs release and expression. Allow yourself to weep and wail, scream, shout and cry and whatever you need to do to let it out. Then select one of your tasks and say No to it, delegate it perhaps or simply leave it undone, the world will not come to an end over something that can surely wait a time, while you give yourself some 'compassionate leave'.

Knowing how much we can achieve, whether it is the practical things or, perhaps more pertinently with the energy of this suit and this card, what we have the will and drive for, can be a key lesson to absorb when this card appears. We all have limits and during a time of Grief, they might shift from what is normal or usual for us. There is no shame in this. Indeed it can point to a certain wisdom and strength of self to be able to admit, to both ourselves and others, when we have had enough and can do no more, and decline an offer or refuse an apparent requirement.

I have read of this card recently that it can point towards the place between guilt and resentment, and that there can lie our 'happy place' (see the excellent 'Tarot for Change' by Jessica Dore).This might apply in the context of Grief. We can have guilt, simply for still being alive, or for any number of reasons connected with the deceased. We may also have resentment, again that the deceased has died, or perhaps with all that it seems we now have to deal with, not least our own broken being.

Finding the place between these two polarities can be a matter of kindness to ourselves. Know that it is ok to feel some guilt and to sit with this for a time. Our resentment, is fine too and we can acknowledge and own it. Once done, we are free to let these things go when we are ready, discard the mountain of wands obscuring our view forwards, straighten up a little, and make a comforting fire from them.

PAGE

The majority of the myriad number of books on Tarot available these days tell us that the Pages represent the youthful spirit, the child-like approach and the long-term view and approach to things. In the case of the Wands Page these traits may all be there, as well as something of the 'inner child' as it is called, the part of us that can direct aspects of our being stemming from unhealed childhood events and trauma.

In the context of Grief we can apply the energy of this Page in different ways. First we can look into what the experience of losing our loved one has done to us, our view of the world and our self and life. This may be especially needed if it is our first (major) experience of Grief. The loss of someone close to us, that we love (present tense deliberate – we do not stop loving them just because they died) – can have a souring impact on us and our beliefs. In the case of the death of someone young, and sudden or violent death, this can be more so.

We may have previously held to a more innocent belief that life is good and that all things work out for the best. This approach may be called into question now, because the inexplicable death of our loved one does not feel like it fits with this and this can leave us with something we do not know what to do with – an energy within us that threatens to laugh in our face at this world view.

And yet, just because we may not feel it so much now, it does not mean that the world is not the nice place we previously thought, or that people are not basically good and kind. It may be that we just need to be reminded that this is what we believe. We can again put pen to paper and write the basic, core beliefs we have that give us a child-like energy that informs our actions and approach to living. To turn to the oft-quoted 'Desiderata': 'Despite all its sham, drudgery and broken dreams, it is still a beautiful world'.

I include this deliberately here, partly because the Desiderata is something I have known for many years and because my daughter Laura gave Amy and I a framed scroll of this, which hangs halfway up our staircase and is hence seen daily. I found that I needed to remind, or perhaps even convince myself again, that my belief in what it tells me, still rings true, as indeed it now does.

Digging deeper, this Page may be guiding us to connect with the child within us and see what they are doing, how they are responding to and dealing with the Grief. There can be an aspect within our being that has known death in some way but did not or could not articulate a response or know how to respond at all. Now may be a time where we can give it a voice and outlet. Even if we did not encounter death in anyway whilst young, there can still be an inner child response that can rise to the surface now. This may stem from any number of childhood experiences where we did not have what we needed fully, in whatever way.

One way we can hear the voice of that child, or that youthful spirit spoken of above, can be to have a conversation with the Page, which can be done with all of the Court cards in their context. On paper, or by recording, we can begin by introducing ourselves, and reply with the very first thing that comes to us, by way of the Pages' reply. Do not filter or check this at all, even if it seems to make no sense. Let the conversation continue as it will, until it feels right to stop. Look back at it and see what has happened and what it might tell you. Let the Page guide you to the enthusiasm and love of the child again.

KNIGHT

The energy of this suit can be exemplified in this card and the stage of Grief that it represents. With the double dose of Fire that comes from both the Knight and the Wands, it is easy to see how this can manifest in Anger. We have identified through the cards of this suit that this is an energy that may surface in different ways, perhaps ranging from a sense of dissatisfaction to all-out fury.

Wherever we might feel ourselves to be on this scale, it is likely that to one degree or another, the experience of the death of our loved one has left us with some kind of response that can come under the banner of Anger. For myself, this is one that I find difficult to get in touch with, simply because I have not fully experienced it, after any of the deaths I have experienced. It takes much to make me truly angry, and usually this is directed at myself when it does happen!

The anger I can feel can show itself more as depression, a different stage of Grief, yet related here. Anger can be one of the basic human emotions, a raw state of our being that we each experience as we do, there being no better or worse way or method. The appearance of the Knight may be signaling to us that we do need to get in touch with our anger and see how we might need to respond.

The Knight may be telling us to question what our anger is, how are we sensing or experiencing this and what we want or need to do with it. In this line of questioning he makes the assumption that we have anger. There is a difference here between being angry and having anger. It is important in saying what we are here, that we do not need to invent anger where there is none, or force anything that we are not ready to encounter. Asking ourselves this question can enable us to get in contact with this fire inside us and give it an outlet and expression that will not result in chaos or destruction, which it often can if expressed unchecked.

A common proverb that is associated with this card is 'Fools rush in where angels fear to tread'. Our gallant Knight knows no such fear and is ready to spring into action at a moments' notice. Whilst this is not always the wisest course of action by any means, there can be great merit in identifying what is required, what is needed in a situation and simply doing it. The energy here is uncomplicated in this respect, direct and with no room for doubt. When the Knight of Wands rears up for you, consider if there is something you need to just get on with, to stop putting off and act.

The energy of this card is abundant with motivational energy. This is not in the sense of the motivational speaker we end up wanting to punch (or is that just me?!) but in terms of a zest for life, an inner drive that once lit can become a burning passion for whatever it is focused on. I have mentioned before how, first with my Mother's death, but each one I have experienced since, one of the conclusions I had was to get on with my life and throw my energy, time, blood, sweat and of course tears, into what I really wanted to do – and here I am doing just that!

The great Henry David Thoreau told us that he went to the woods to 'live deliberately . . . and not when I came to die, discover I had not lived'. The Knight of Wands does this, and some. Now may be the time to consider how you might turn the energy within you from your Grief into a powerful driving force that allows you to live as deliberately as both these noble figures.

QUEEN

We have seen that the inner energy of anger we are dealing with in this suit is not limited to that state alone. It can manifest in many different ways and can be fueled from many different sources. The Queen of Wands is adept at either caring for her own needs and loving herself or completely neglecting them. Her appearance may be suggesting that you need to consider this for yourself and consider what needs of yours may be being neglected.

It can be all too easy in our Grief to neglect the things we need, and ignore those things that keep us on an even keel. This may be eating, drinking sufficient fluid (not just alcohol if that is your thing), sleep, rest, communication, sharing and so on. Another list may be called for here, where we write the things we know we need or usually do as part of our routine in life. We can then see which we are doing, to even a slight degree, and which we are completely neglecting.

It is important that we do not give ourselves a hard time over what we are neglecting. The Queen is of the heart as well as Fire and as such knows she needs to be compassionate with herself. So here we can look at ourselves fondly, forgive ourselves if necessary and know that it is understandable and perhaps to be expected that we may do, or rather not do, such things. We can then turn to our list and see which is the most important and begin to do something about it, in however small a way that may be.

One of the chief attributes I feel this Queen has is that of knowing herself very well. She has the ability to look into her heart and know its truth, its core, what causes the blood to pump and what motivates it. It may be helpful for you to consider this in yourself when she appears for you - to look into yourself and ask what it is that now drives you and pushes you on, in the fire of your Grief. Bringing this into our awareness can add a layer of strength and self-knowledge that may have been obscured. In the intensity of Grief it can be as if we are plunged into the core of the fire, where we can encounter what it is that keeps us going. Knowing this we can gain something that is truly unassailable.

The energy of anger can also be one that tends to blind us to other needs. It is not that we wake up every day and immediately feel a raging anger burning our blood; more that there is a varying sense of what could be called disillusionment, malaise and dourness about us. Being in touch with the heart, this card is the Queen of dealing with this, almost like parenting the sulky child. Her energy can be that part of us that tells us it is ok, expresses empathy at the sense we have, and looks lovingly into our eyes, knowing that we will rise above this, as we tend to the spark within us that is still lit.

KING

The King is exemplary at getting down to brass tacks. The intellectualism of his fire can be directed at the basic truths and tenets of life. It is when we are exposed to something such as death that we are faced with the raw essence of our existence, and our own reason for being.

The King does not ponder the meaning of life in an existential way. Rather, his focus tends to be inward, concerned as he is with the inner force of why we do what we do, what we believe that causes us to be who we are and live the way we do. His view is that it is not so much what we do but the reason we do it and the manner in which it is done that matters.

His appearance can suggest that we need to look at these traits within ourselves, in the light of our Grief and the different approach to living we may sense as a result. I have mentioned before how significant turning points such as the death of our loved ones can impact us, and here the King is counselling us to consider our direction in life anew.

This is not to suggest that everything, or indeed anything, must change. It is only that it can be wise and helpful to re-consider our being and our life in the light of this shift we have experienced. The death of a loved one is a shift, in one way or another. The appearance of the King can be telling us to check in with ourselves and see what we are sensing now.

Concerned with the truth of our existence as he is, the King can also be guiding us to look at discarding anything which no longer sits right with us. He can perhaps see beyond the force and energy of the anger we may feel, and see instead its root and what ignites it. He may see whether we are being true to ourselves and that an adjustment may be needed to bring us back into alignment.

Burning away that which is no longer true can be a case of shedding our defenses. The anger we term as such can be an effective shield against the rawness we may need to encounter. Grief can bring us into a direct presence of the raw truth of (our) life and it is easy to want to recoil. Anger is a way of doing this, and in various different ways and means. As we begin to see the spark that keeps our inner flame alight so we may be more able to release ourselves from the shields of our defense mechanisms, however they might manifest for us, and open ourselves to who we truly are, what we really know, and what we are actually here for.

Knowing this, the King tells us to focus on connecting with these aspects of ourselves, and use the fuel within us as a response to our loss and Grief that allows us to live in accordance with the knowing and awareness that comes from this connection.

PENTACLES - BARGAINING

ACE

It is interesting that in the most common depiction of the Aces in the Tarot they are offered as a gift – in the palm of a hand emerging from a cloud in the case of the RWS deck, like some kind of divine benediction. I see these as the gift of each of the aspects/faculties of the human being that the structure of the Tarot places for us – our inspiration, our thinking, our feelings and our actions.

In terms of the process of Grief, in the case of our actions and our behaviour as they are depicted in the suit of Pentacles, it is something of the opposite. It is as if we look for some kind of divine placation through what we do.

It can be easy to see the stage of Bargaining as taking the approach of doing a deal with the divine – if I do this, will you keep them alive/bring them back/dull the pain. But the Bargaining we can indulge in can be different to this. Each of the above three motivations are seeking to avoid something – the death itself and/or the pain as a result of it.

Yet we know that death is the one thing in life that can never be avoided. Delayed perhaps, or even advanced, but never avoided. By seeking to see our actions and behaviour as in some way redemptive, we immediately create an impossible scenario for ourselves, doomed to failure from before the outset.

So there seems no point in pursuing such a goal or target. What happens then if we return to the idea of the Pentacles - our physical being and what we choose to do with it – as a gift from the divine? We can see our physical, everyday life as the vehicle for our Soul and how we can therefore best lead our lives in light of this.

In this way we can, despite the abject pain and even horror of the loss of our loved one, consider what we might be able to learn from the experience. This is not so much looking to find the good in it, in a 'Pollyanna' kind of way, but more of a determination that it will not beat us down, or leave us hard, bitter or angry for the rest of our days. Rather we can resolve to become more of who we are, lead a life of purpose and meaning, and of following the longing of our Soul through what we do with the rest of our life.

That process can begin with the appearance of this card. This is what can be on offer for you now. We know that we do have freewill, so in this knowledge there is a time we can choose to apply that in a way that lays a foundation for a future in our lives that will see us spending our time and efforts in a goal that really means something to us.

This may be 'easier said than done' of course, and yet when we consider many of the great achievements in history, very few if any, came without great effort, determination and often a foolhardy belief in the seemingly impossible. I am an easy example of that - for many years I wanted to write a book, any book, I had no idea what about, I just wanted to write one! This is my 10th.

TWO

Each of the Twos in the Tarot can be about Balance, in their own area. In the case of the Pentacles Two this can be a need to maintain a sense of balance in our everyday life, in our behaviour. This may mean avoiding extremes – over or under doing it.

If we bring the idea of Bargaining into this concept, then we can see how we might take the attitude in our Grief of the 'payoff' - conducting a negotiation with life, the Universe, the Divine or whatever. We may be projecting, either through what we do and how we do it or through our speech, the proposal that if we act in a particular way, or carry out an activity, the result will be that we feel better about the death we have experienced, or will experience.

In the energy of this card it can be all about creating a scenario of life in which we are safe, where we are in control of the outcome, because we have made a deal that tells us this. This is of course a fallacy and so the need with this card can be to accept that such things as loss and death are beyond our control, they are bigger and stronger than we are and we often cannot predict them.

We cannot be fully in control of or measure our process of Grief after the event has happened. So the energy of this card may be carrying a message to allow us to 'go with the flow' more in our Grief, to accept that our very being and sense of self may be out of control for a time. It may be that one day we have abundant energy and we do much, yet the next day we spend our whole time in reminiscence of our lost oved one, crying over photos and music and so on. All of this is fine and it is just what we need to do at that time and on that day.

It can also be said that there is an energy inherent in this card that tells us that all things will in the end, come to balance. This is not said in a condescending 'it will all be ok' manner, but one that assures us of the workings of the Universe. It is rather like the concept of the Yin/Yang symbol that reminds us that there is in everything good and positive a little darkness, and vice versa. So we might like to remind ourselves that how we are now may not be how we are tomorrow, next week, next month and so on.

Eventually we may come to the conclusion that it is only ourselves that can begin to create how we are going to be in our future self by what we do in the present. Once we can begin to realise this, and also accept that we cannot be in control of all outcomes and workings of the Universe, we are able to be part of that natural Universal flow that is part of the beautiful evolution of all things. In time, we can begin to enjoy the ride once again.

THREE

When we look at the numerological energy of the Three we can see how it illustrates the principle of creating something – in the case of the Pentacles, something tangible, and doing something constructive in our situation.

The traditional image of this card is of an architect, sculptor and monk, within a church, as if they are in a planning meeting. These could equate to different aspects of the self and the dynamic creation that can emerge when we consult with them and allow their voices to be heard, then acted upon.

When in the midst of Grief it can be easy to either separate ourselves from the outside world and 'go it alone', since we may feel like there is no-one that can truly know our pain. That may be true but to be helped we have to allow it to happen. If we do not permit our self to open up just a little then we do ensure no-one can reach us and help us, let alone actually be there and help us do what is needed.

Each of the aspects of the self illustrated in the card has a function – the architect to help us design a plan, the sculptor to show us how it can be done and the monk to help us understand why we need to do it. So it is that the 'bargaining' of this card can need to be made with ourselves.

We can see the church that this scene is taking place in as representing the 'safe place' we may have retreated to, often in a literal, physical sense. This is a natural response to the feeling we have in Grief – a need to be somewhere known, familiar and 'cosy'. Yet there can come a time when we need to see that we cannot stay there permanently if we are to grow and flourish in our own life.

The appearance of this card can suggest that we now have a need to consider what it is we are creating by the actions we are taking now and the behaviours we are engaging in.

We may perhaps be building a place that is a safe haven and that is fine, for now. However, we may need to consider the long term impact as well. It has been said that change is the only evidence of life, so it can help to realise that at some stage we will need to move out beyond those safe and familiar comfort boundaries we may have put in place or are doing so now.

Much as in the present moment we may not wish to, it may be that we need to heed the voice of those different aspects of our self, whether they come from our own mind or, as can be quite common, those of others who are reaching out to us, asking us if we would like to visit somewhere.

As we know only too well, after a loved one has died our own life can never be the same again. Given this, and despite the enormous sense of loss, pain and fear this might have given us, this card may be asking you what the new and different life you need to create will look like.

FOUR

Here we have the card of the miser, the one who likes to grab hold of everything that he can and cling on to it. I have always thought it highly significant that the figure holds a pentacle across his heart and so his heart chakra centre. This becomes like a shield, something that prevents him engaging with his own feelings or those of others, preventing him from being reached and reaching others. He is also situated apart from the town, in 'splendid isolation' as he would have it.

In our Grief we may take to being this way - anything to escape the pain and be safe. I am writing about Grief in the sense of a loved one having died since I am writing from a largely personal perspective, but of course we can experience Grief in many situations. The end of a relationship forced on us can be one such apt example here, where we can carry out certain behaviours to shield us from pain and loss.

The energy of Four in this card can be about stagnation, staying put and refusing to budge. This may well be necessary and even helpful for a time as we look to a recovery from what may initially appear to be the misery of our life and existence now. Yet, we do know, somewhere deep within the deepest well of our being, that 'nature abhors a vacuum' and that nothing can continue to exist inside such a state for a long period of time.

When this card appears it may be suggesting to us that it is time to come out of hiding, to gently, cautiously and with all due caution, poke our heads out of the tortoise shell and have a look around. How does the world look like to us now? What would happen if we were to set foot out the front door? We may not want to go far but we could take a brief walk down the street and back, or even to the nearest shop, even buying ourselves a treat if we felt brave enough.

There can be an obstinacy to this card, rather like the horse that pulls up before a jump and will not go forwards, no matter what. We may well be justified if we are acting like this, not wanting to go out or do anything much, let alone try something new. Yet we cannot deny the evolution and the life-force within all things and the Universe itself. Sooner or later, something will inevitably shift and the practicalities of our life must respond.

This card may be asking us to consider if that time is approaching, whereby we can act before the Universe does. When looked at in a context such as Grief and from any kind of therapeutic context, many cards ask questions of us. Here, it may be something along the lines of 'You can't stay like forever, what are you going to do next'?

The boundaries we may have erected for ourselves, physically and practically, consciously or not, can serve a purpose and a valuable one. When this card appears we may need to consider whether that purpose has been fulfilled and is now outmoded, even to a small degree.

FIVE

This is one of the images that when we are in Grief we may readily identify with. The standard image of the two figures, struggling along, one on crutches, in the wet and the snow, can be a good summation of the sense of abandonment and existential existence we can have following the death of a loved one.

These two unfortunates in the card are usually shown outside the warm and welcoming light from a church, the stained glass window of which features the five pentacles. The suggestion here is that what they need is within reach, they simply need to choose to go in.

When we are dealing with our Grief however, this may feel like an impossible task, and even something we do not want to do. We may be engaging in a bargaining game that says we should not go after what we need because it goes against the sense of loss and suffering we have. This can amount to the idea that if our loved one has died, why should we have any happiness?

I have learned, both in my Grief after a death and a loss or situation that has shaken me to my core, to address my immediate needs. This may initially be on a moment to moment basis. I may begin my day with some tears as I cuddle a pillow in bed. Then I need a drink, next to hear a human voice (TV/radio), then clothes and so on. If need be, just existing in this way I know will get me by. I have deliberately put these things in the context of being physically alone, even though I am not, but it can certainly feel like you are.

Later, it may be that I can move to sectioning the day into parts - before breakfast I need to do this, in the morning I will do that, the afternoon this and so on. It can then move to day to day, and gradually to bigger projects and longer terms goals, as things unfold and as I feel safe and secure doing.

The emphasis here is on the practical, and this can include all the others since this is the outcome of the inner energy of our being and our existence. This suit is about the practicalities of our life and our behaviour. Here it is as if we are doing a deal with the world, the bargaining aspect, that by doing something that we know we need to we will not create a demand on anyone; we are doing our bit for the Universe and it will keep us safe.

It can be that the opposite can apply when we receive this card. It may be that we are, again consciously or not, avoiding that which we know we need. If this feels familiar to you, then consider the last time you ate, the last time you had any (decent) sleep, the last time you gave your body some attention, the last time you went outside of your home and so on. Make a list of at least these basic needs and resolve to respond to each one in turn, at least one per day, as you go forwards from here.

If you feel bad or guilty when you begin to do so, or consider doing so, you may like to turn the bargaining to a positive use here, by affirming to yourself that you owe it to your lost loved one that you need to be looking after yourself, addressing your own needs and giving yourself what makes you feel good. In time you can once again do those things you like for yourself, and in this way honour the life of your loved one.

SIX

The image here reminds me of the many things that need doing and dealing with when someone dies. There can be much to sort out, in terms of dealing with officialdom and the legal demands that must be met; the funeral itself, plus whatever social things might follow this, the personal possessions, the deceased's will and so on and on. It can seem that everywhere we turn there is something to do, somewhere to go and someone to deal with.

There can also be other people, those around us who have needs and demands too, as they each seek to respond to the death of someone and respond in their own ways. All of this will be dependent on both our own and others situation and positon in relation to the deceased person, so we may need to place ourselves in context here.

In the middle of all this, is our Grief, which has its own demands and needs. So the first thing to consider when this card appears may simply be whether we are giving any due concern to our own needs. Please notice the use of the word first in the previous sentence! In this I am reminded of the pre-flight instructions given on airplanes - should the oxygen masks drop down, put yours on first before helping anyone else – you cannot of course help anyone else if you have passed out.

Once you have seen to your own immediate needs to keep yourself going then it may be that you can consider others. Here we may need to be mindful of what we do and how much we do it. When in Grief it can be easy to be too reliant on others, whether giving or receiving and it can be useful to consider when helping becomes rescuing.

It may also be that we ourselves need to ask for help. Consider if this cards' appearance is signaling that you need to reach out and ask someone to help you – whether it is spending a little time with you to ease a painful evening, share a meal, or even cook one for you, accompany you to a place that you know will be difficult, or help you with one of the many things that require seeing to at this time, in the wake of the death of your loved one.

The act of sharing at a time of Grief can mean so much and giving even a little can give so much to the recipient. At different times or on different days we may be the giver or the receiver. This is where the sharing can be a beautiful and healing experience, again, both in giving and receiving.

We often hear of the need in business to 'speculate to accumulate'. In the context of Grief this can also apply, not necessarily financially, but practically. There can be an understandable reaction to want to hold onto all of our loved one's 'things'. Of course there will and should be some that we keep and treasure. There can also be many that others could use, or wish for themselves, so it may be worth considering this part of the practical necessities when this card appears, even if it is just the acknowledgement at this point that it will need doing one day.

SEVEN

One of the strengths I find with the Tarot is that it can offer us choices and options. For me, working with the Tarot is all about empowering the user, so offering us options in our present situation enables us to begin to create the outcome and future we want. This card can illustrate that very well for us.

There can be two ways of seeing the usual image for this card. It can be the person who has completed their days work, or a project, and is pausing to take a breath and see and feel the satisfaction that comes from looking at what they have produced. Equally, it could be the image of someone who has so exhausted themselves from their work and toil that all they can do now is lean heavily on their staff to support them.

When we are in our Grief, it can be easy to assume the latter of the two here. Grief can be an extremely tiring and draining process, coupled with the disturbed sleep we may be experiencing. Add to this the seemingly endless number of tasks we have to do, and we can end up willing to bargain away much for a decent nights rest.

There can be no denying that many of the tasks that can need to be done arise both from the death of our loved one and the inevitable pile of things that can mount up that we have put aside, delayed or ignored whilst we deal with the more immediate demands of our Grief. These things can happen whether we are directly involved with funeral planning and so on or not.

The task with this card can be to turn the second of the two above choices to the first, where we use the blood, sweat and tears of the tasks required to create satisfaction and even reward for ourselves. It can be incredibly helpful to first make a list of what needs to be done, from the small, seemingly mundane things to the larger projects.

We can then more easily prioritise and begin to have some kind of control over that we are doing, and a level of understanding why. In this way we can actually make a bargain with ourselves. As we are able to tick off an item from our list, so we can give ourselves a reward, or if that does not feel good, a recognition of having done something. What form that takes is entirely up to you. It need not be anything extravagant, or potentially harmful (over-indulging etc.) - it could be a favourite food, a soak in a bath, watching a film, chat with a friend and so on.

There is a great practicality to this card – seven is the number of the Earth level of our existence, so can manifest simply as 'getting things done'. It can therefore be about our evolution, or our progress through life. That may all come to seem pointless in the aftermath of the death we have experienced, and yet we cannot simply press a delete key or pause our own lives and do nothing.

In the emptiness we may have, both inside our body and soul and outside in our everyday life, we can choose to see a rusting wreck or a fertile ground. If you find yourself wanting to choose the wreck, consider first what your departed friend would choose for you.

EIGHT

One of the books I have read to help me deal with my own Grief focusses on finding meaning in it. This card brings that to mind. Here we see a figure carving out the last of eight pentacles he has produced. We can assume he has been at it a long time and his focus seems to be fully on his task. When I see this I find myself asking why is he doing this?

We can assume it is because it is his job, and he will make some money from it. This is his meaning. We can also hope that he derives some satisfaction from what he has achieved as well. We can translate this to the process of our Grief by looking at what our lives are now that this has happened to us.

In essence of course, nothing has happened to us, it has happened to our loved one who has died. And yet, that nothing can also be everything. The death of a loved one can cause us to reframe the whole of our life from that moment on. Everything can look, feel and actually be different. That which had meaning and purpose before may no longer do so. What we strove to achieve and put our effort into, gave of our energy and self to, may not now have a motivation from within us.

In the last card we saw how the Bargaining with it can be with the self, and it can be the same here. From my Mother's death over 30 years ago and my daughter's death this year, every time I witness, however close or distant the death of a loved one, or a public figure I admire, I am reminded of the transient nature of our life and the reality of my mortality – the fact that I will die and every day it is one day closer.

This is not said from any place of morbidity but of motivation, of determination to make my life have meaning, to myself first and hopefully to others – so if you are reading this book and it has done this for you, write and let me know!

The poet Dylan Tomas famously told us to 'Rage, Rage against the dying of the light'. This is what I like to see this figure is doing. There he is at the end of the day, still working hard at what he has chosen to devote his day to and he has produced perfected work he can be fully satisfied with. He will gain both an inner and outer reward from this, a pay out from his bargain.

When this card appears for us, perhaps we can consider the output from what we are doing and even give some consideration to why we are doing what we are. It may be that very little, if anything, needs to change in our outer, practical life, or it may be that an overall shift and change is required, to bring ourselves into alignment with the new goals, targets, and motivations and urges we have in the wake of the loss of our loved one.

NINE

This is often the card of material prosperity and achievement, with its depiction of a richly clothed lady, surrounded by all the trappings of wealth and finery. The term 'trappings' is used deliberately here, since it can be that we become trapped, or at least restricted and blinkered by the material path in life. Indeed, that seems more and more prevalent in our modern world, to the dismay of myself and many of my generation.

Of course a direct encounter with death is a stark reminder that you 'can't take it with you' as John Lennon said. Of course it is next to impossible in western society to avoid the need for money and we will always have at least basic physical and practical needs and there can be nothing wrong with some comfort and lovely things.

At the time of writing my wife is about to begin her second round of chemotherapy treatment, a cancer tumor having been found in her adrenal gland and her brain. Throughout her course of treatment we have been given stark reminders that the aim of treatment is not a cure, but to prolong her life and keep her as best she can be. For us, this is the reality we have learned to live with, and brings 'preparatory grief' high on our priorities.

Because of this the material message of this card can seem quite laughable. The focus for us has become sharing the time we have and with our loved ones, as far as is possible, whilst making the practical and necessary adjustments to our lives that become required. In this way I can see in this card a message of making the most of what you have got, as well as looking beyond materiality.

As I look at the card what also comes to mind is how the lady on it is focused on her activity. She is gazing at the hawk on her arm (or whatever bird it is meant to be!) and her attention is fully focused on what she is doing. She is in 'the now' as the trendy saying goes. There can certainly be a reminder here that all that truly exists is the present moment, and perhaps the love we have within that moment.

When this card appears following the death of a loved one, I see here a reminder to *live*, to enjoy the time you have, to be grateful for the time you had with your loved one, to see the good things and the beauty the world has. Even if in our Grief all appears black and dark, we can still look at a picture of a beautiful sunrise, or whatever we find inspiring and of beauty.

Many Tarot commentators draw our attention to the snail that is making its way quietly and unobtrusively across the foreground of this image. In Grief I think this can show us the need not to rush through our life, but to truly not need or want that much, certainly avoid greed and exploitation, and instead just go about our business with humility and a quiet determination to achieve our goals. In Grief the knowledge that life is short is all too fresh so let us respond to that knowledge.

TEN

Here we have a card that shows the different generations of what we can assume is a family, gathered together. They have much - a lovely house (castle in this case!), good clothes, money and so on. And yet, all things must die, as we will know only too well in our Grief.

There can be a clear communication in this card to be sure that our material possessions and 'affairs' are taken care of before we die. This may seem trite, and yet the practicality and necessity of this cannot be over-emphasised. When the Covid pandemic began my daughter wisely took out a life insurance policy, given that she worked for the English NHS and was dealing directly with covid patients from the outset. Although covid did not feature in her death, her life insurance paid out and thus avoided a great deal of consternation and difficulty for her widowed husband and their two boys. When my wife was first diagnosed with her incurable cancer, we both made out our wills.

Another feature of this card has always been the arrangement of the pentacles in the 'pattern' of the Tree of Life. In this I see ultimately a depiction of the descent of life-force or energy, from the source (god or whatever) to its manifestation in the physical, the domain of this suit in the Tarot. The zig-zag direction this takes is known as the Lightning Path. In this I am reminded of the saying from Teilhard de Chardin that "We are not human beings having *a* spiritual experience, we are spiritual beings having a human experience".

In Grief we can suddenly be faced with the direct mortality of our existence and what can seem an apparent pointlessness to it all. We can see this reflected in the simple numerological energy here. I have often described the Ten as there being something and then nothing, one and then zero. It is the ultimate release of the physical and the practical in this card.

Whilst this card has its image of plenty and abundance, it also seems to me to point us towards looking beyond all that, to consider, what is its point and purpose and what then is the point and purpose of our life? In the light of your Grief you may be able to consider what the point, purpose and direction of your life is now that this sad shift has occurred in it and within you.

The figure of Death has been called The Leveller (in the poem by James Shirley) and in the context of this card and our Grief we can see that this is so very true. The apparent trappings of life, the never ending quest for more, money, possessions and security count for naught as far as Death is concerned. I think that the older figure in this card knows this and is content instead to feed his dogs, quietly enjoying the time he has with his family. When all is said and done there is little of more value than the relationships we have.

PAGE

At the imaginary entrance to the Court of Pentacles we first meet the Page. They are the earthiest of folk, given we are in the suit of Earth and I associate the Pages with Earth elementally. This can result in their having great plans for what they will do and achieve in the world, but can be so very slow to actually do it. They are certainly the tortoise rather than the hare!

This can seem quite strange since in many of the cards in this suit the focus I have taken is on living, after the death of our loved one, on garnering our focus and acting and living like every day could be our last. I have spoken elsewhere of how I have long had this motivation and lived my life to make the most of my time. Many years ago a close friend asked me what my first thought was each day and my reply was 'What can I achieve today', something I still do in fact, though it may take a little longer to get round to the thought! Incidentally, hers was 'What fun can I have today', something I must ask her if she still does. Both these approaches would be good medicine for our erstwhile Page to apply to themselves, and if they have appeared for you, perhaps the same applies?

When we are dealing with Grief everything can seem like a huge effort, and we can become very much like that tortoise. There can be a reluctance to move on, perhaps due to not wanting to leave our loved one behind. Even though we know our own life goes on and we cannot stay exactly as we were, still we might resist the natural evolution and progress of our life. It can be that without knowing it we are trying to strike a bargain with the world or the Universe, that if we stay as we are we will not forget our loved one and their memory will stay fresh for us. This is a fallacy however, and deep down, we know this. But it can be natural to grab at anything that gives us comfort and security when we are deep in Grief.

Another aspect that comes with the energy of this card is being presented with the reality of all that there can be to do following a death. This has been touched on before, and here it can be about the not doing of it. I have often thought that the mantra of the Page here is 'mañana, mañana', meaning that tomorrow will do, no need to rush.

It may be that we need to tell ourselves this or adopt this attitude to some degree if we are feeling under great stress and pressure to 'achieve', to get everything done that needs to. This being the case we might benefit from listing all that we know needs doing and choosing one to do – tomorrow.

Of course we may find ourselves at the opposite end of the spectrum of energy of this card. In this case we may be doing nothing at all, and using our mañana mantra as an avoidance or delaying tactic, trying to sidestep what we know is really inevitable. If this is how we find ourselves, the same exercise as the one above can be useful, just ensuring that we do actually carry out the task we have assigned ourselves first. Applying mañana in this case can be a way of easing into action, and keeping the Page's tortoise pace. Either way progress can be made and we can begin to move towards the vision of our future life, even when, as is often the case, we cannot see one right now.

KNIGHT

One of the oft remarked on features of this card is that he is the only one of the Knights not to be moving on his horse. He is clearly prepared to do so, in full armour and with the visor on his helmet raised so he can see what is ahead. Atop his strong and impressive looking horse he has a good view of the landscape he is in.

When we are in Grief we can feel as if we cannot see anything ahead other than loss, sadness and pain. It is often said that time is the healer that is needed, but this can offer scant comfort when we know only that we are feeling a huge loss and yearning for our loved one now. Nothing else seems to matter at this time.

As one day moves into another the intensity of those feelings may lessen but the core of them does not, and arguably, never will. It may be the case that we get used to that sensation within us and that the 'healing' referred to here is simply knowing what that feeling is and that this is our 'new normal'.

When this card comes for us, what can matter may be that we acknowledge that this is how we feel right now and allow ourselves to be open to other feelings coming into us as our life does indeed move forward, as surely it must. Notice here that the suggestion from this Knight is not to remove or obscure the feeling of loss in anyway, but to ask 'what else might there be'?

The very fact that the Knight is on such a strong horse can also provide us with a productive and therapeutic symbol. It can be true to say that for the vast majority of us, there are sources of help and support available as we go through the process of our Grief and that we are only ever truly and fully alone if we choose to be. We can consider that the Knight is asking us what is supporting us and list those things. It may be a list mainly of people and if so, how wonderful and fortunate we are to have this in our lives, as are they to have us in theirs.

By way of example, my list following my daughter's death includes – my wife and (other) daughter, the Tarot and writing this book, being in natural places, living near the sea, exercise in various forms, meditation, losing myself in 'binge-watching' TV series, my garden - and more. This brief and incomplete list reminds me that when I step back and look at it that my life is not all about Laura's death, or my wife's illness, but things of learning, creativity, challenge and beauty.

In my way of Tarot, the Knights have the energy of the element of Fire within them. For this Knight, it tells me that, though for now he is still, he will act when he senses the time is right. His very nature does not allow him just to stand there forever, but a force within him tells him that he must move onwards and continue his quest.

It may be that seeing ourselves as a Knight on a quest seems like an outmoded fairy-tale for the modern world, but for me it can serve as a wonderfully motivating idea and energy. You might find it helpful to indulge this fantasy and see yourself as the Knight, planning the next stage of his quest and ask yourself 'what is there for you to find and treasure'?

QUEEN

In this card the Queen appears to be gazing adoringly at the somewhat large pentacle she cradles in her hands. She is on an intricately carved throne, in a beautiful landscape, dressed in luxurious clothes and with a crown on her head. She is the epitome of luxury and beauty.

This may seem hard to relate to when in Grief. It can certainly feel that the beauty, pleasure and general loveliness has left our world, along with the person who has died. The Queens for me are of the heart, having the elemental energy of water within them. This means that they can empathise with others and in the case of this Queen, will show this by their actions.

It may be that the Queen of Pentacles comes with a challenge, this being for us to recognise the beautiful things still in our life and the world. Certainly it may be and feel like the main source of that has gone, but we can instead begin our ubiquitous 'therapy list' as we might call them, with the memories we now have. The questions the Queen now has for us is 'where is there beauty in your life' and 'what is it that you value now'?

The appearance of this card can also offer us an opportunity for some self-therapy. When we are in Grief one thing we can be sure of is that we 'have been through it' as the colloquial saying goes. We may still be 'going through it' and this process may not cease for a while yet. Can it not be the case then that we have earned and deserve some kind of reward, or if that idea and concept is too much, then a simple acknowledgement of what we have done so far and will keep doing, in terms of keeping going, if nothing else.

When she appears the Queen might suggest to us to do something that we love, just for a short time. This might be as simple as buying yourself your favourite chocolate bar (or bag of crisps in my case!), visiting a favourite location, watching your favourite film or whatever appeals. Knowing that whatever you choose to do you are doing so because you are at least recognizing that your worth can be a powerful reminder that the spirit within you is still serving and guiding us, and will do so for the rest of our life. If you are struggling with this another and helpful way of looking at this can be that we see it as a gift from our deceased loved one.

This Queen is a lover of physical beauty and beautiful things in general. If nothing else, by way of self-help when she comes calling for you, you might choose something that your departed loved one admired for its beauty and do something to recognise this. Perhaps it was a particular place which you can visit, or get a picture of, a person you can read about or watch, or whatever seems appropriate for you. The act of honouring this beauty and love is in itself a way of honouring the person who has died and reminding ourselves that beauty and love still exist somewhere, somehow, in our lives.

KING

I have always thought this King somewhat odd looking but there is no denying his standing in the world and lofty position and air. He is dressed so richly and manages to appear cool, despite apparently wearing armour under the rich and heavy looking robes he wears. He holds his symbols of authority and status and seems to exude an air of knowing and surety.

His surety can come from knowing what he is doing. The combination of the elemental energies of Earth and Air give him a practical wisdom that assures him he can work it out, whatever it may be and arrive at a solution. If that turns out to be wrong, in whatever way, he will re-consider and come up with a different answer.

His approach requires a certain detachment and it is here that we can learn something from him in our Grief. It can of course be so hard for us to step outside of and beyond what we are feeling and knowing when we are trying to deal with and respond to the death of someone we love. The hole they leave behind may be the limit of our vision at this point. We can then use the help of an outside voice, and the King of Pentacles, with his detached, practical wisdom, can be that voice.

We can either write or record a conversation we might imagine having with the King whereby we simply start by introducing ourselves, and come up with his reply, and do so without stopping to consider and think about it. Rather we let our intuition prompt our words, looking at the King as we do so. You do not need to know 'what this card means' or anything about the Tarot for this to be productive, and in some ways, that can help!

Here's a sample beginning of mine that I will create now –

Steve – 'Greetings Lord King. I need some help'

KP – 'With what do you need help'?

Steve – 'My daughter has died and I grieve her loss so much. What can I do to help myself deal with this pain'?

KP – 'You might describe that pain, give it a voice and a persona. You then might have an ability to step away from your pain a little when you really need to and see it instead in this other person'

Steve – 'Thank you, that sounds like it might be good when it is really hard. I can imagine what that person might look like. It's as if I feel them as an angry part of me, which is odd and I haven't really felt anger about this before'.

KP – 'Perhaps you can allow that anger to speak and find release from it, without the need to cause harm to any other in anyway.'

This brief beginning has already shown me an aspect to my grief that has not surfaced yet, and given me a method of bringing it to the surface in a way that feels both manageable and productive. This is not something I had considered or envisaged in anyway before this was just written.

CUPS - DEPRESSION

ACE

Although this card is connected with the Depression stage of Grief we need to not make the mistake of thinking that when the Ace appears it indicates the beginning of our depressive state. We need to realise that the use of the term depression here does not need to relate to this in a clinical sense, but the process of what I call 'facing and embracing' our sadness and emotional state in general.

The appearance of this card can then suggest to you to consider first what it is you are feeling. It can be natural to respond first to this suggestion with the sadness, guilt, loss, yearning and pain that can be seen as the hallmarks of Grief. Not to brush over these in anyway at all, or to belittle their strength, impact and power, but it can be that we do feel other things as well, even if just for glimpses and short amounts of time, in the early stages at least.

It may help us to identify those things that bring us anything that is not a sadness or depressive feeling. We might write those on a list to place on our fridge or mirror to remind us of what it is that can alleviate our pain and show us that there is still some pleasure to be had in life. As we move forwards we may even be able to give ourselves something that could result in something enjoyable.

The path through the emotional fallout that comes with Grief can begin with first recognising what emotions and feelings we are having and in so doing honouring them. This card may be as simple a thing as reminding us that we are allowed to be sad, to cry, to miss our loved one and all that they meant to us. This may seem an obvious thing but there are times when we need to give ourselves permission to feel our emotions fully and do justice to them in this way.

As can be seen from the symbol of the dove that is seen descending from the top of this card, it is ultimately a card of healing, that process beginning with the energy that this card can bring us. As a healer myself I would also recommend receiving some healing while we are in Grief. The trauma and sometimes shock of a loved one dying, even when it may have been expected can still be huge. A session of healing from a qualified healer can help to soothe the energies of your being which in turn will help promote well-being at all levels within you.

An initial response here may be that you are not ready for this, or even that you do not want to be 'soothed' or even 'well' at this stage. Rest assured that healing cannot make you experience anything you are not ready or willing to have. The whole session can be carried out in silence if you wish, ensuring you do not have to confront or express anything you do not yet wish to.

When teaching Tarot I often explain that for us to be healthy and whole, we need to express our feelings and emotions. Like water, if they remain stagnant and unexpressed, they become polluted and poisoned, and will manifest as such within our body, usually where we may be weakest physically. The appearance of this card might be asking you to get in touch with whatever it is you are feeling and let it out.

TWO

The Two of Cups is often viewed as a card representing relationships, connection with someone and love in general. Clients are often pleased when they see its image appear, as two people toast each other, gazing into each other's eyes, while the healing caduceus image appears above them. As with other cards, this may appear to be at odds with the Grief process.

There are however, two ways we can work with this card as part of dealing with Grief. First, we can see each of the people in the card as representative of our deceased loved one and ourselves. Although this can clearly be a painful and emotional thing to do, the energy of the card can prompt us to focus on what there was, and in some senses, still can be, between our loved one and us, rather than on the loss and the pain of separation.

If we are feeling such pain following their death it follows that there must have been many good things we shared with them. This card can suggest that it is good and healthy to recall those things, be aware of them, nurture them, even celebrate them and in so doing we may come to realise that the love we had for them, and them for us, can live on. Of course this does not have to be applicable in only a romantic sense, but in whatever way our relationship created that love and which we experienced and shared.

As we look at this card, it can be easy to see the figures as exchanging cups. When we feel able, we can move on to seeing how we can carry that love forward, and see it as a still active energy in our self and in our life – as if it is a gift from our loved one that we can use and apply. The message here being that although they have died, the love has not. I have often maintained that love is the strongest energy in the Universe and that energy cannot be killed or die. This card can bring a healing focus to what might otherwise be only sadness.

The other aspect I often illustrate to my clients when this card shows up for them is that it can be about our relationship with ourselves. In this sense I see one of the figures in the card as the client, the other as their mirroring reflection. In Grief, this can also be taken as an opportunity to focus on something positive within us, rather than only on what we have lost and is sad about this time.

Do be aware that in suggesting this I am not downplaying the sadness, heartbreak and pain of the loss, or suggesting that we should ignore, sidestep or avoid this at all; quite the opposite in fact. The energy of this card is the sharing of the energy of love and this can come as a timely and needed reminder, amidst the potentially dominating force of our sadness, that we have love in our lives still.

You may, again, find it helpful to list those things – the love of a partner if you have one, your friends, family members, pets, the love you have for your favourite music, films, and so on. Love can manifest in so many ways, each unique and wonderful. It can be a healing thing in itself to sit and think about, then list, the ways that there is love in your life.

Then consider whether you included yourself in that list? If you did, how far up were you? What is needed to increase you love of yourself? If you did not include yourself, why not? What is needed for you to begin to learn to love yourself?

We can then see how we can express those things through our lives, seeing the love we had for our loved one as a springboard for the time remaining to us on the Earth as an opportunity to further the unfolding of the love we had for our deceased person.

THREE

Following on from the Two, this can be another of those cards where it can seem difficult to relate what we see to dealing with Grief. The standard image is of three women who seem to be partying, raising their cups in a toast and enjoying the spirit of the moment. When in Grief, this can be the very last thing we feel like doing.

There has been a noticeable trend in recent years for the concept of a funeral to shift to one of a celebration of the life of the person who has died. Whilst this can have many positive aspects to it, there is a place and a need to feel the loss and to fully mourn for that person. As such, the funeral can be a time to begin this process collectively, and such shared rituals can be very powerful on many levels.

Equally, the celebration of the loved one's life has a place and also fulfills a need. The appearance of this card may be asking you to remember to do this and perhaps consider if you have done so as yet. After the funeral of my closest friend, now many years ago, two other friends of hers and myself, who had not seen each other for quite some time, decided to go the local pub. There we reminisced about our friend, shared some laughs - and several pints. She'd had loved it, she was that kind of woman. It was not a bittersweet occasion, it was, if not quite a celebration, a memorable pleasure.

Whilst it can be a very sad thing to ruminate over the memories we have of our loved one, doing so alone can easily lead to a deepening of this state – especially if there is alcohol involved. I see in this card a call to gather with some of those who knew the dead person and to meet socially, in whatever context, for the express purpose of sharing memories. Amy and I, along with her sister and others, speak often of Laura and I find this not only a lovely thing to do, but a healing one. For certain they are tinged with sadness at the very least and open tears too, but the strongest energy again, is that of the love we have for her and she for us and all that she was in life.

There is the 'old saying' that it is at times such as this when you find out who your friends really are. There is something of a presumption in that though, that such people will be knocking on our door, calling our phones, or more likely now, posting on our social media, to check in with us, offer help and so on. Such care and selfless love really does make the world such a better place. However, my sense is that it is also up to us to reach out when we have need, rather than sitting at home and allowing the sensation of the victim to creep in, reminding us from the back of our mind how no-one bothers us now, does not *really* care and has forgotten what we are going through. I have always been something of a natural Hermit, and am quite happy in my own company and yet feel so blessed to have so many people I can turn to should I have need and who I know would be there for me, day or night.

The appearance of this card can suggest to you to consider if you have a need to reach out, for whatever reason, for solace, company, reminiscence, or sharing a bottle of something good. Perhaps, if you truly are alone and have no-one to connect with, it can be time to acknowledge this and seek help with it. In Grief, I see this card as turning depression to love, or finding love within depression.

FOUR

Here we have the epitome of the stage of depression that this suit connects to in the Grief process. It usually shows a downcast person sitting with their back against a tree, gaze down towards three cups in front of them and either ignoring or not seeing a fourth, often shining cup being offered to them from an unseen or known hand – usually interpreted as 'the Divine' or an angelic being.

In contrast to the previous two cards, this is an easy image to identify with Grief and one that we may visit repeatedly as we navigate the five stages of our process. As with all cards however, there can be different ways to view what we see. The initial response is that the person in the card is not seeing there is help being offered, that they literally only have to reach out and take the cup to get what they need and want. Instead they seem to prefer to keep their gaze at what has gone before and, in terms of Grief, see only the sadness of the death they have experienced in their life.

Or we could assume that the person in the card has drunk the contents of the three cups, has had their fill and therefore chooses not to take the one being proffered. They may well know it is there and can see it perfectly well, but is content as they are, indulging themselves in the moment as they feel is right for them. Either way, it is their choice.

The energy of the number four of this card can be about security, and one of the strong emotions we can experience when experiencing Grief is that of the loss of what was stable, safe and known in our life. The death of someone close to us can shake the foundations of our life and cause us to feel vulnerable, threatened and insecure.

It can be that the first response to this card that we need to consider is what is it that we are feeling in the moment;

what is our need right now? Do we need to indulge ourselves and cry, letting some healing tears flow for the loss of our loved one and the hurtful pain of life? Or do we need to realise that we are feeling a sense of fear and need something, or someone, to help us with this? Or is it something else we are feeling that is causing us to be like we are at this time?

Either way, when this card appears for you, it can indicate a need first to root yourself in the present in this way, to ground yourself through what you are feeling to the present time and place. Once there, it can be asking you to consider how you need to respond to those feelings, whatever they are. A valid question posed by this card can also be whether there is something we are choosing to ignore about our Grief process, or refusing to see or acknowledge, when deeper down we know what it is that we need.

An aspect of this card that can be easily glossed over can be the significance of the tree the figure is sat against. It is tall, straight and in full leaf. The symbolism here is that, perhaps without knowing it, the figure has given themselves exactly what they need – a place to sit and be, a source of strength and power, of rootedness and protection. The appearance of this card may be suggesting for you to find your place to sit, and be.

FIVE

It could be argued that this is the card that carries the quintessential message that drives both the motive of writing this book and my work with Tarot as therapy. I have found it is another of the images that clients identify with when it appears in their readings. Clients tend to have readings when things are not going well for them or they need help. The beginning to uncovering the energy of this card for most people is to ask what this figure needs to do.

The fairly simple answer to this is for them to turn around and focus on the two upright Cups (the figure is apparently seeing only the three that are spilt). There can be more to this process if we dig a little deeper however.

Firstly, it can help to identify what it is that is currently being felt and to know the apparent causes of this. In terms of Grief this can seem to be easy to answer – the death of our loved one. Yet it we look deeper we can consider what it is we have lost ourselves in their death. As tragically sad as it is that they have died, we can remind ourselves that they are now OK (depending on your belief system of course) and have left any pain, suffering or trauma behind.

So what we have lost can be what it was they brought into our lives. It may help to come up with three factors that were the biggest or strongest things we feel they took with them – their sense of fun/humour, the time we spent together to . . . and the chats we shared, for example. Next it can be good to look at two things that we now have, still have or can choose to continue, though they are not with us now – maintaining that fun/humour in our approach to life, ensuring we always have someone to confide in and vice-versa.

In short, this card can be about recognising the emotional values and pleasures we have lost, and allowing ourselves to weep for them. This can be followed by seeing how those things can endure the loss and how they can contribute to our being the best version of ourselves we are able to be going forward from here. In this sense, it is a way of honouring our loved one. Just as the card is set at night-time, it follows that another day will dawn and the Sun will rise again.

We can see the bridge in the background of the card, crossing over the river, which we can symbolically see as the 'rainbow bridge' between the worlds carrying our loved one over the river Styx. There we stand, grieving our loss, seeing only ruin and feeling only despair. The figure is cloaked in black, yet we cannot see what they may be wearing beneath. At Laura's funeral suggestion was given for people to wear green if they wished, this being her favourite colour, which many did, often with some black too. In colour symbolism, green can be a colour of the heart and healing, two traits entirely suited to Laura. You might like to ask yourself that if the figure on this card represented you, what colour would you wear beneath the cloak?

SIX

This is traditionally the card of nostalgia, childhood memories and something of the innocence of the childlike state emotionally. Whilst the idea of nostalgia is an easy one to grasp in relation to Grief, it is less hard to adhere the other two aspects to it.

Taking the concept of nostalgia first, there can be something of a soothing, healing balm in allowing ourselves to recall the times and memories associated with our loved one. After Laura's death Amy found great solace in sifting through hundreds of photos of Laura that we have – so many expertly taken by her sister Kate – and sorting then into different 'albums' on her pc, then selecting those she wished to have printed and placed in frames and physical albums. Once completed we had a treasure trove of memories and images of our beautiful girl and Amy had processed a portion of her grief.

Care may need to be taken in such tasks so as not to slip into wallowing. Amy did admirably in moving on from this when she had done what she needed and wanted to, then engaging in other tasks. Nostalgia can serve a healing function as part of our Grief, but we need to ensure it does not develop into something more like the sulking child!

In turning to the 'child' aspects of the energy of this card, we can look to the concept of the inner child in relation to Grief. This is the part of us that has always been present, in our subconscious, and as adults retains the position of our child self – whether it be the feeling of security from a parental hug, joy from a grandparents gift and so on, or the fear of being left somewhere, the hurt from being 'told-off' and so forth.

For the vast majority of us we cannot and/or do not give voice to, or address the feelings we have as a child, and so we internalize them. There they stay and as adults we can act these out as programmed responses to external stimulus. The experience of Grief can be a powerful trigger to stimulate such wounded feelings, as well as an equally strong opportunity for healing.

I personally found working with my own inner child incredibly helpful and healing, if at times quite hurtful and painful, in revisiting some of 'Little Steve's' senses. The work can run deep within us and it may be that the help and guidance of a qualified professional may be sensible and required. For those wishing to begin to explore this subject I would recommend the works of John Bradshaw.

For now, you may like to ponder on the feelings you are having in your Grief and cast yourself back to any memories these might stir for you from your childhood. It can be helpful to describe the circumstances to someone, allowing yourself to almost become that child again. By identifying the source of such feelings you can gain more of an objectivity over them, loosening their hold on you and at the same time helping you deal with this part of your Grief process.

This can be deep work and may not be for everyone, but if it resonates with you as you read this, it may be that the energy of this card is showing you the hand of your little self, outstretched for you to hold.

SEVEN

This has always struck me as something of a curious card, and in my experience the same is true for a great many clients when they see it. It shows a silhouetted figure who is gazing at seven cards floating in a cloud, each cup with a different symbolic object in it, be this jewels, a castle, garland and so on.

I have often been asked what each of these symbols 'mean' or represent. My response is usually along the lines of 'what do you think they mean'? The idea here being that what each of us sees in them is what they mean, to us. This translates equally well to our emotions when we are processing Grief.

Given that this scene appears in a cloud, we can relate this to our imagination. This is not to suggest that we are imagining what we are feeling in our Grief of course. We can though, give ourselves easily to wanderings in the mind, fueled by our feelings, whatever they may be. We can use this tendency to further our therapeutic efforts as part of our Grief process, and to help deal with what is here classed as the stage of 'depression'.

It can often be the case that when a loved one dies, especially so when that person is still 'young', or we perceive the death as premature, we are left with ideas, plans and desires that are unfulfilled and will now remain so due to their death. We can see the symbols in the cups as each representing one of these. It can be helpful to create a list of those things - perhaps seven in this case - and let us ourselves engage in a little fantasy wish-fulfillment.

We could then visualize ourselves, with our loved one carrying out those tasks, or simply imagining what it would be like. This needs to be done at a time and in a state of mind and heart when we are receptive to the pleasure and lift we can obtain from this activity, rather than it being a source of further anguish. If this cannot be done, then this exercise may not be right for you, at least yet.

Alternatively, (or in addition), we can carry out an activity, as appropriate, that we had planned with our loved one, as a means of turning a fantasy or unfulfilled wish or desire to reality, and as a wonderful way of honouring our loved one and their life and our shared plans. There is nothing wrong with telling your deceased loved one about your plans before you carry them out, and afterwards, describing your visit and so on.

A further way of working with this card can come from the fact of the figure in it being in silhouette. It can therefore represent our lost loved one, as well as ourselves. We might then imagine our loved one looking at each of the symbols in the cups and considering what they would make of them and what they would do in response to each of them. We can list these seven things and alongside each one record their (imagined) response. We can then do what seems right and appropriate with the information we have created.

EIGHT

Chief among the concepts for this card is the idea of emotionally 'moving on'. This can relate to leaving behind an emotionally draining or unproductive situation or relationship. As such this is one of those things to which we can justifiably respond with 'easier said than done', and especially so in the content of dealing with Grief.

I have found that whilst it might be productive to leave my Grief behind, it is not something I can just do, or make happen. More than this, there are times when I actually do not want to move on from it I want to dwell in it, so I can feel it fully and thereby know I have got to its roots and core. Only then can I truly move on, knowing I am not dragging its detritus along with me.

In the card we see a figure who seems to have turned their back on the eight Cups and is creeping away in the still of the night, guided by the Moon. The scene suggests to me that they are following an inner instinct or prompting, and may simply be putting one foot in front of the other, with no real idea where they may be headed or what the results of their actions may be.

Yet something within them tells them it is right to do so. When in Grief sometimes all we can do is get through the day and, literally or metaphorically, put one foot in front of the other. We may feel abject despair and the stultifying horror of our loss, but we still have to keep living our life one way or another. Even if it is a case of 'fake it till you make it' the energy of this card reaches out to us to hold our hand and lead us gently onwards.

I am often struck by the arrangement of the Cups in this card. Despite there being the number eight, they are not arranged evenly as one might expect in two rows of four. Instead there is a gap on the upper row of three Cups. Through that gap is where we see the figure taking their moonlit walk. In this sense, they become the missing factor that restores equilibrium and balance to the scene. When in the depths of the depression of our Grief such qualities as these can be hard to grasp, or even have a sense that we will ever come to know again. This card seems to me to have a suggestion that even in things which are not as they should be, there is still beauty, and love.

The figure has a staff in hand, with which to aid their walk and which helps to prop them up, especially when the going gets particularly tough. The metaphor and symbolism here is not too hard to grasp in relation to our Grief – we may just need to identify what the staff is for us in our life when the card appears, and make use of it.

Beyond this, my sense is that what is causing this response in the figure is something deeper than a desire to leave the cause of their upset behind. The Moon has an effect upon us that reaches beyond the logic of our mind and deeper in, to our instinctive or intuitive responses. This can cause us to do things without fully, or even partly, knowing why we are doing so, only that it 'feels right'.

In terms of Grief, the energy of this card may be telling us to accept that even though we do not know how or why, we need to follow those inner promptings and see that the world keeps turning and that our life continues to exist and evolve after the death of our loved one. When we look deeper we can perhaps come to a sense or even realisation that, as we follow those inner prompts, we can have a sense that moving on will cause things to be ok, and it is the right thing to do. For now, this may be all we know, and all we need to know.

NINE

As Nine is the highest single digit we have it can represent the peak of pure energy numerically. I often look at Nine as the product or outworking of 3 x 3, where the three is the creative force of the Universe. This creates the best we are able to be at the time, the most we can strive for and the peak of achievement.

In the suit of Cups this would suggest the energy of this card brings with it an emotional pleasure, satisfaction, or a 'high'. All things, once again in this suit, difficult to relate to when we are dealing with Grief. However, we can need to place this in context, the key phrase from the paragraph above being 'the best we are able to at the time'.

The chap on this card looks quite chuffed and satisfied with himself. The requisite Cups of the card are arranged on a shelf behind and above him, rather like trophies of his emotional achievements. For me they can act like a shield, not in the sense of a wall we can hide or take refuge behind while we wallow in our Grief, but the strength we can derive from the very fact that, despite the terrible loss we have experienced, we endure and keep going.

It may help to identify what those emotional strengths are for us at this time. The energy of this card can for me be about 'emotional intelligence', whereby we can step outside of what we are feeling, even just for a few moments, and identify what it is we know to be true in our self and life that helps us endure this loss and pain.

These may be different for each of us of course and they can even differ from day to day. In my experience it can be at such times of Grief, and the pain that comes with it, that we can add to our store of emotional intelligence and strengthen our stock of wisdom, resilience and resolve, emotionally speaking, When this card turns out for you it can be good to question what yours are, and if indeed you can come up with Nine, you can perhaps feel a sense of quiet, humble, inner satisfaction like the man in this card.

One of the things I have also experienced from my responses to Grief is that, after some time has passed following the death, there can be a galvanising impact, chiefly on my emotional self. With each death I have experienced in my life it seems to cement the sense for me that life is transitory, really can be all too brief and that we need to press on as best we are able and try to get everything done that we want to.

In order to do that we first need to know what it is we actually want to do. To begin this card I spoke of the peak of achievement and the most that we can strive for. When this card appears it may be bringing with it a need to acknowledge our as yet unfulfilled desires and a call to respond to the things in your life you have yet to do, but really want to. For me, I see in this a means to honour the person who has died.

It can be all too easy to prefix our desires with a conscious or unconscious 'one day I will . . .'. The energy of this card can be about this day, now; and the emotional fulfillment we want, made all the more poignant and meaningful following the death of our loved one.

TEN

With regard to Grief, a casual glance at this card can provoke a similar response as we can have with the Three in this suit, especially so if the death we have experienced is that of a family member. It seems to depict 'happy families' to me, a couple arm in arm saluting their happy home while their children play happily at their feet. It seems to epitomize domestic bliss.

Yet the numerical energy here for me is all about letting go, of dissolution, the Ten being the one followed by the Zero and the culmination giving way to the inevitable. Perhaps this is why we have two generations depicted in the scene.

One of the things I feel that the times of Grief I have experienced through my life have shown me, is that nothing is guaranteed, permanent or 'forever'. The exhortation to 'expect the unexpected' can be a useful one to keep in our heart, not in a morose or negative sense, but one which tells us that placing our security in anything other than the impermanence and surety of change, is foolhardy.

The various chops and changes of my life, some expected, some not, some welcome and some not, and some initiated by me, others not, prove testimony to this approach to life. The searing pain of Laura's sudden death and the incurable nature of Amy's illness (I cannot bring myself to write this relating to death in anyway as yet), are my most recent and current and wholly unwelcome proof and reminders of the principle. In many conversations forced by our situation, Amy and I have said repeatedly 'if you go before me', since however likely it might seem now that I outlive her, we cannot really know. What happened to Laura proves that.

The energy of this card can then be an exhortation to live for now, live for the moment, or, as the now cliché goes 'carpe diem'. But what exactly does that mean, and how does it relate to our dealing with Grief? Firstly I would suggest it asks us to feel what we are feeling, not to shrink back from it, but let it be expressed and in so doing, find a measure of sweet release from it. Of course in terms of our tears and pain, this may keep happening, and that is all part of the process.

Beyond this, I feel the energy here can prompt us to look at what is still beautiful and good in the world, in our own life, and in ourselves. We may not immediately feel like there is any, but if we dig deeper we can find there is still love around us and still love within us, submerged at present beneath the pool of our tears perhaps, but there, quietly and patiently placid, ready for when we are.

As difficult as it may be to feel in some moments, even impossible, the energy of this card can remind us of the rainbow that appears in the darkest part of our sky. Following the energy of the Nine in which we saw a re-focusing on our emotional desires, the energy here is one of exhortation, of beginning now, of converting the pain of loss and grief to motivation to live, more truly and freely than before.

PAGE

This Page is staged before what appear to be quite choppy waves, which he has his back to, perhaps fortunately. He holds a cup aloft, out of which a fish seems to be coming! Somewhat of an odd symbol, this is traditionally seen as representing the emergence of psychic and intuitive abilities. In general the Page of Cups is taken to be a youthful person, romantic and poetic, and often not a little ungrounded!

This can seem almost the opposite to what we might be feeling when experiencing grief. It is noticeable that there is nothing between him and the water, and just a brief step back would see him plunged into its depths, showing us that when he appears for us, we could be that close, not to drowning in our feelings, but certainly in danger of being submerged at times, bobbing this way and that in those waters.

The Pages are usually seen as young people, and as such we can make a link here to the possibility of not really knowing what we are feeling as we try to deal with our Grief. It can be that one day, or even one minute, we feel ok and reasonably calm, all things considered. Then, perhaps stimulated by something we see on TV, read or hear, we can be set off on an emotional roller-coaster as another part of our Grief appears, like the fish out of the cup.

It could be easy to draw analogies here with maxims, or clichés, such as 'not swimming against the tide' or 'going with the flow'. Whilst these may suggest good approaches to take in our Grief, the Page seems untroubled by such things. His attention is solely on the fish in his cup. From this my suggestion is that his guidance for us would be to look beyond what we are feeling each day, each minute and each moment. Being by nature a person of the heart he understands and knows within that any feelings that come to him will pass, flowing away with the next wave.

Deeper within him, he senses that there is a knowing within his being that beneath the surface of his turbulent feelings that sweep him along, there is a place of greater calm. This is what we can look to in our Grief, knowing that the feelings and emotions we experience will pass as we release them and our sense of self that somehow tells us everything will be ok, will return. It is this that I see the fish as representing in this card.

It should perhaps be made clear that this is not to decry or suggest avoidance or suppression of depth of feelings, whatever they might be. If anything the opposite is true. Through their expression and release our feelings are there, and then they are not, and we can come back to the place of calm, precisely by the full release of our emotions (appropriately, where required).

The Page tells us to feel what we feel, to dive right into it, then emerge, dampened by the water perhaps, even soaked, but then restored and becalmed, our feet once again on the kind Earth.

KNIGHT

Our erstwhile Knight of Cups looks as though he is setting out on his latest quest, in full armour, his horses head bowed as if they are presenting themselves to their King and Queen before they depart. He holds his cup as if in offering or toasting the royal couple and receiving their blessing for his quest.

The Knight is a figure of passion and he loves nothing more than to devote himself to something, a worthy cause or person to whom he can offer undying allegiance. He is, if somewhat romantically unworldly and impractical, someone that once he has made his dedication, will stick to the principle of this, come what may,

In Grief, it can often feel as if our life, sometimes suddenly, is bereft of all meaning and purpose. Everything can seem futile, when we are presented with death before our eyes and in our hearts. The futility of all that we seek and strive for can hit us and motivation for anything can plummet.

The Knight may have appeared to be of help to us with this. He is a combination of the energies of both Water (from his generic suit and type) and Fire (from his status as a Knight). As such the blend can produce passionate dedication, as well as understanding, which he can first offer us.

Knowing how we feel, the energy of this card can carry a message to look for honour in life and in that honour, see a quest to which we can dedicate ourselves, perhaps for the rest of our life. This could perhaps begin with considering how we can best honour our deceased loved one. What things in our self and our life can we do to honour them and to what can we dedicate ourselves to continue that process.

On the morning of the day that I write this I watched a news film of a man who in a wheelchair, and with the support of his worthy team, climbed Mount Kilimanjaro and reached the summit. He was paralyzed through spinal injuries after a terrorist bombing in Manchester Arena in the UK. Another member of his team did the climb in memory of his wife who had died. He could not reach the summit, but the dedication was still there.

Though we see such charitable enterprises often these days, and they are all hugely inspirational, not all of us have such a calling. Indeed it may be that our quest begins with getting outside, if just for a few minutes, perhaps for the first time since our loved one died. Or eating a full, nutritious meal. Perhaps we do resolve to support a charity that connects us to our loved one in some way. For me, it is the writing of this book. For Amy, it was a renewed dedication to fight the cancer, when it could have been so easy to give way to resignation in the aftermath of the death of our daughter.

In the stories of the quest for the Holy Grail, the Knights are asked 'Whom does the Grail serve'? We might ask ourselves 'what can we serve', this becoming our own personal Grail.

QUEEN

The Queen of Cups is such a creature of water she could easily become a mermaid! Belonging to Cups she is 'of water' and her Queenly status gives her the same attribute. This tells us she feels everything and this is her modus operandi for life.

With regard to Grief this can be both a blessing and a curse. When she appears for us, she may be indicating a need to look at what we are feeling, to ensure that we do not become overwhelmed by our emotions, as can be all too easy to do at such a time. We may know that our emotions will pass, that they can rise and fall and can often be something 'of the moment'. It can be helpful to allow them to be expressed, to avoid suppression or denial. Equally, it may be that we need to maintain a degree of objectivity now and then, so we are not becoming so submerged in what we feel in each moment, as our Grief dictates and gives rise to, that we lose a sense of reality and truthful perspective. This can be part of this Queens counsel.

Her other guidance can be regarding empathy. When we are in a state of heightened sensitivity, the world can be a difficult place to traverse. When our Grief is raw and we feel exposed and vulnerable, as is an inevitable part of the process at times, it is easy to be swayed this way and that by every emotional stimulus we are given exposure to. This can be music on the radio, scenes on the TV, stories we read or hear and so on. Each seem perfectly aligned to cause a spike in our emotions, and off we go again.

Going outside of our home, which can often be something of a challenge when in Grief, we are exposed to a myriad of potential emotional triggers. It is not that we necessarily look to empathise with everyone we encounter or pass by, but our innate sensitivity and simple raw vulnerability can cause emotional reactions that we would not normally or otherwise experience.

The Queen understands this and may suggest that we make whatever allowances we need to for such times. There are no rights or wrongs here, only that we each respond as is right for us and our own needs and wants. Some of us may need a trusted companion with us if we go out, to help us if and when overwhelming emotions strike, while others may prefer to be alone. A helpful approach can be to simply ask ourselves 'what do I need right now', as we experience these emotional tides and waves.

I have said often that the key to successfully navigating and using the energy of this card is loving the self. When we operate from a basis, not of self-centeredness or selfishness, but of simply loving ourselves, then all that we do is infused with this, and it naturally extends out to those we encounter and interact with. We are empowered to give of our best, and are not belittled or made less by our actions and interactions.

Learning to love ourselves can be a big task. Looking back, I know I did not really or fully do so until sometime in my mid 40's. An effective self-assessment can be to draw a line down the middle of a page and list the things and ways that show you do love yourself on one side, and the things and ways that show you don't on the other. When you then review your list, take a loving and compassionate approach, rather than a harsh or critical one. Pick one of the 'do' list and celebrate it, and one from the 'don't' list and find a loving response to it.

KING

Having written in the last card about how the Queen can show we may need to regain some objectivity with our emotions, the King can exemplify this, with his elemental combination of water and air. This combination of heart and head respectively can blend to give him an intuitive sense that guides him to his truth.

When we are experiencing Grief, accessing our intuition can be a seemingly impossible task. We are often told that we need to 'quieten the mind' and/or still the heart in order to feel and know our instinct and intuition. When Grief is rampaging through our self and life, a quiet mind and calm heart may be what we crave, but can remain tantalizingly or painfully out of reach.

There are techniques we can use to help – such as imagining an energy flow up from our heart and down from our head, to meet in our throat. We can allow ourselves to open our voice box and let out a sound, whether a chant, or an 'aum' or maybe just whatever noise comes to us to make. This can really help to connect us to our truth, and freeing the energy centre at our throat can help us express this. Chanting can also be valuable just by itself, for much the same reason. There are many chants available to us, and my recommendation would be to use whatever feels right for you.

The appearance of the King of Cups can suggest to us that we need, one way or another, to look at what our mind is telling us and what our head is telling us. It can be that he comes to ask us the questions 'what are you thinking' and 'what are you feeling'? It can help, to gain a perspective on these, to make yet another list – this time on one side of the page we can list our feelings and on the other, our thoughts. This can be in general in our life at this time, about something specific – our Grief or any aspect related to it, or about a specific moment in time where we may be struggling with Grief for any reason.

It can also help to look at the interplay between our head and heart. It can often be the case that we are having feelings and emotions as a reaction and response to what we have been thinking. The opposite can also be true, where we may be thinking in a certain way because of what we are feeling at that time. The King may be coming along to show us that the truth, or what we need to know, realise, or see is in the blend between the two. So his counsel can be to avoid extremes, of feeling and thought, and instead look for compromises and blends that bring us to a place of balance, by which is meant calm and peace within.

These things can help us to arrive to a place where we 'just know' what is right for us. We may not be able to reason, explain or justify this to somebody else, but the point is that we do not need to do so to anyone, only ourselves. So long as this does not cause harm to ourselves or others, we need only to sense it is right. How do we know this? Because we do.

THE MAJOR ARCANA

THE FOOL

Many approaches to the Tarot posit this card as the 'ultimate' card. The Fool can be seen as the epitome of the Tarot and its teachings, encapsulating in his being the essence of what it is to be human. The Fool can be representative of the ideal of being true to who we are, in every moment. He lives a life free of limitation, doubt, worry or restriction of inspiration, thought, feeling or action.

In all this he can seem to be something of an antithesis of how we are in our Grief. It can be easy to think and feel that we will never again be able to return to a sense of lightness and freedom in our self and life, such is the weight and burden of the experience of the Grief process.

It could help to make it clear that the lightness of The Fool does not come from a lack of concern or engagement with life and what it brings to him. The huge challenge he sets for all of us comes rather from his ability to accept what happens to him and retain that lightness of being regardless of what this might be. This includes Grief, since this is a guaranteed part of our life experience.

The Fool is sometimes referred to as being naïve. Let us not mistake this for ignorance. Instead he has an instinctive, or perhaps cultivated, ability to take what he encounters and effectively absorb this into himself, transmuting it into his being and becoming a part of him. In so doing he is able to fully 'face and embrace' all of life's joy and beauty in equal measure with its tragedy and despair.

If the challenge is to take our Grief and allow it to become a part of us, it can be both a seemingly insurmountable task, and a simple, almost instinctive one. If the energy of our Grief is to be a part of us, it means that we have to reach a stage of full acceptance of what has happened; the death of our loved one, and to do so in such a way that does not allow for residual acute pain or anguish.

I use the term 'acute' here deliberately, since the acceptance can come from accepting all that is associated with the experience of our Grief – happy and cherished memories, if now bittersweet, as well as moments/times/days of sadness and tears and all else besides. All are allowed to move through our being with equanimity and no resistance. In this lies the acceptance of this stage of the Grief process and that is aligned with the Major Arcana cards.

There is a quality within The Fool that tells him that whatever he experiences in each moment will pass. In knowing this he can accept it and in so doing it becomes a part of him and he can then release it, thereby keeping his innate sense of freedom of self and lightness of being. Nothing he experiences, thinks, feels or intuits defines him. It simply 'is what it is' and is then released.

With regard to Grief this does not mean The Fool will not feel the full gamut of emotions we associate with it. Rather he can allow himself to feel everything, as something he is experiencing, something that is happening to him in that moment. Beyond this there is his being, and this provides him a baseline of peace and wellness that is his essence.

This is why dealing with Grief can be both the heaviest of energies and tasks, and a simple, instinctive one. When we can accept that Grief is a part of 'life's rich tapestry', however we experience it, apart from our individual tragedy, it can be possible to begin to see life beyond, or not defined by, the death of our loved one and the loss of them in our lives.

It is perhaps something of a cliché, but still a truism, that Grief is all about us, not the person who has died. If we believe in any kind of 'afterlife' or spiritual existence other than our physical one, then we can have a sense of knowing that our loved one is fine. Grief is therefore about us, and our adjustment to the absence of that person in our life. There is something in the spirit or quality of The Fool that allows him to keep the awareness of peace within his being. This can come from knowing that physical death is part of our existence and experience.

For me, I have found that despite the loss of my parents, best friend, teacher, daughter and all too swiftly it would seem, my wife, I have to believe that life is still an amazing adventure, that the world is a wonderful place to be and that people are essentially good and loving. Without this, I see no point in existence. This is what I see in The Fool and which both helps and guides me through my Grief.

These losses have each become a part of my existence and experience and each has had their effect upon me; how could it be otherwise? But none have defined me, or I hope and think, limited me. If anything they have motivated me, taught me and improved me. There will always be such a sadness but that is OK. My belief/knowledge is that I will encounter these souls again, which comforts me. In this I can find the equanimity of The Fool and still be open in my being to experience all that life can offer me – love, joy, laughter, as well as pain, loss and anguish. Each has their place, each is an energy and a part of me, yet none defines or limits me. In this I find solace and peace.

THE MAGICIAN

For a long time now I have seen The Magician as someone who is engaged in the task of learning how to be a human being. The four symbols on his altar, equating as they do to the four Elements and Minor Arcana suits, are also the four levels and aspects of himself, and of course, every human being. By way of reminder, these are the physical, emotional, mental and spiritual.

As this is the first numbered card of the Major Arcana I see the Magician as being engaged in the first, or primary task of his humanity; that of learning how to navigate, use and control these four energies and abilities. This is putting the task somewhat simply, since there are many subtle and delicate aspects to what is involved in the interplay between his senses. He needs to learn that each has its function and role and none must be allowed to dominate, the requirement being a balance between them all. Once this is achieved, then something of his and our magical nature can be expressed.

I pointed out early on in this book how Grief is something we can all expect to experience, death being perhaps the one true certainty of life. As such, we can see it too, as part of the task of what it is to be human. Applying the same approach of the Magician to his task, we can see that our Grief can impact every level of our being.

The physical effects can be felt in many ways, from its impact on our sleep, our appetite, our physical energy levels, and an apparent decrease in our immune systems function, leaving us more susceptible to picking up such things as colds and bugs we might otherwise shrug off. In Grief, it can seem like our bodies are under attack.

Emotionally we can feel all over the place of course. One moment we may feel quite stable and smile at a fond memory of our lost loved one, but the next minute someone says something or we see or hear some other trigger that instantly has us in floods of tears and sobbing. All are fine and a natural part of the process.

Mentally we can be equally prone to ups and downs. We can each be prone to different triggers at this level, just as we are emotionally. Our need may be to learn to recognise those things that cause us to plummet mentally and take action to consider avoiding such things, at least for a time. In tandem with this, we can also become aware of what lifts us up and feeds our mental health and ensure we have a good intake of them.

Spiritually the impact can be experienced through our motivation, which can fluctuate wildly in Grief, as well as in things such as questioning any faith we might have, or belief in whatever spiritual approach we usually follow. We could be angry with the deity we follow or worship or find that we cannot engage in our usual spiritual practices, be they prayer, meditation, ritual or whatever.

All these are ultimately an individual practice and as is the choice of how we need to respond to them, there are no wrongs or rights. I feel that what The Magician is showing us is that we need to become aware of our Grief on every level of our being, seeing each one as a part of our whole. In doing so we can learn to control our Grief, rather than it controlling us. What this can mean is that we can allow the impact to flow through us, do its thing, have its effect and then come back to something approaching balance. In short, we need to let go of control, in order to have control!

Put another way, control is not suppression, it is in fact the opposite. By letting ourselves experience and express what we need to at each level of our being, we can learn to recognise that we do not need to be fearful of our Grief; it does not control or define our being. It has been said that there are only two basic emotions, Love, and its opposite, fear. When we move past the natural and understandable fear that belies some of our behaviours and experiences in Grief, we can embrace a Love made all the more strong, both for ourselves, those around us, and in a now positive way, our lost loved one.

It can be very easy to adopt behaviours and attitudes in Grief that we are expected to take, even without realising we are doing so. It might be that we need to become aware of any ways we are behaving or doing things simply because it is what we think is expected of us, or we feel we should (or should not), or ought (or ought not) do. As we become aware of our own needs in our Grief, so we learn the lesson The Magician appears as our card, to teach us.

THE HIGH PRIESTESS

The High Priestess, depicted usually sitting demurely on her throne, typically represents that part of us that knows, our intuitive self, and the influence of our unconscious. She is the guardian to the inner mysteries and the inner realm that lies beyond our five senses. Having mastered or at least come to know of these as the Magician, The Fool, or The Seeker as I prefer, must now turn inward and come to know this part and aspect of what it is to be human.

For our purposes here, in the process of our Grief, this points us towards what we may be sensing or knowing within ourselves, but have either chosen to ignore, have not acknowledged as yet, or are simply not consciously aware of. We may therefore need to connect to this inner part of ourselves in order to access what the intuitive or unconscious layer of our mind might have to communicate to us.

For this to happen, we will need to 'quieten the mind' and use a meditation or breathing technique to shift us away from the ongoing barrage of conscious thought that can be typical as we try to process our Grief. Sometimes this can seem like an impossible task at such a time. We could then try a bath, lit with candles, infused with essential oils and some relaxing music of our choice playing quietly. We can draw the curtains in a room in daylight, sit or lie comfortably and play our music, letting ourselves just flow with it and see what arises from within our minds.

As we emerge from our reverie we can then write down a 'stream of consciousness', which we can see as what The High Priestess is saying to us. Try not to analyse or even consider the content as you write, just let it flow and let her talk. It can be helpful to then leave this at least overnight, or until such time as we are not thinking about it or can recall what was written. Then we can read and review what was written to us and this can reveal useful insights.

It can be that the language used in such communication is somewhat more symbolic than literal. The unconscious can bypass the logical and rational part of our brain and speak more in pictures, symbols and images. We may need to bear this in mind as we conduct our review and see what associations come to us as we do so from these things.

Sometimes in Grief it is easy to have so many inner thoughts and things going through our minds that we either lose a sense of coherent thought or they just pass through our mind, as we whirl in a continual state of perpetual motion mentally, and often as a consequence, emotionally. I have been told that on average the human mind will repeat the same thought pattern up to 200 times as it seeks to come to a point of understanding and acceptance. That points towards a very draining mental energetic output that we can well do without at such a time.

If we can then observe and perhaps write notes of what our repeating trains of thought are, we can express them and release ourselves from the wheel of what is not being said or expressed. This could take several forms, from the trusted friend we can confide in who will just listen as we speak, to writing something, perhaps to our deceased loved one, saying all those things we never did and now regret, or just need to release ourselves from. In either case, it is as if the High Priestess is asking us 'what have you not said about this that you need to'?

The High Priestess can also be acknowledged as a listener, so her appearance may indicate that we need to either have someone listen to us, or we need to listen to what we are being told. This may be from ourselves, as described, or perhaps to the guidance or suggestion, as opposed to advice, of those who know and love us. There can sometimes be a reluctance to admit to what we know we need to do, or respond to our Grief, and sometimes this can require us to push beyond the veil of our defensive thoughts and feelings.

In all of this The High Priestess can be something of a mirror to our inner self, reflecting that which we know to be true within ourselves somewhere but can struggle to acknowledge and come to accept. In this she has a powerful and valuable gift for us.

THE EMPRESS

I have always looked on The Empress as Mother Earth, in her role as giver and creator of life, and sometimes that which also takes it away. Obviously, both aspects apply here. The emphasis in these applications can be placed on the maternal role she has, in terms of her care for the welfare of others and her natural inclination and instinct to give, of herself and what she has in order to safeguard and protect where necessary and ensure not just survival but flourishing of life.

So often in the writing of this book what has come to mind is how for our deceased loved one the hard part is done. Having left (the restraint of) their physical body behind they are fully restored, free of any pain and suffering they may have experienced at any level and are moving on in the next world, Otherworld, spirit world, heaven or whatever term we like to use. Grief is about us, not them.

As such we can see in this card a need for care. Where and how this is directed can depend on our place in Grief. If we are in what we could call a secondary role, where we know of someone who was much closer to the deceased person than us, then it may be that we need to offer care for them, in whatever way is applicable and appropriate. The term 'offer' is used deliberately here, since it is not for us to assume or force that care where it may not be required, wanted or necessary – the care here is about the recipient, not the giver.

More directly for our purposes here, it may be that we need to look at our need to care for our self. Certainly in the early days of Grief such things as regular eating, sleeping and our normal daily habits can understandably and even necessarily, go awry, whilst we try to take in what has happened and deal with many things we have to and face each one. Indeed, care for the self can be applied as we do these things, taking each one individually, day by day and doing no more than we feel capable of each time. Not letting ourselves be rushed or pushed in anyway, by any other person or authority can also be part of this.

Enlisting the help of others, in whatever way and at whatever level, can be a surprisingly difficult aspect of self-care. Being able to say to someone, 'I have to deal with some financial things today, could you help me', or 'I need to sort their clothes through. I want to do this by myself, but can you come round when I am done as I know I will be upset by it', is a powerful expression of self-care and of self-love.

Attending to our own needs is a vital lesson in life, and doing so first is equally important. This way we are in the best place to give to others, and to do so from a healthy, more genuine position, rather than a needy or wanting one. It is not selfish when we are clear about why we need to do this. In Grief everything can become twisted and reversed, so applying the 'me first' principle can be valuable at such a time.

It can be that one of our responses to Grief is to overly give to others, especially so if we are naturally caring and giving. It can be easy to fall into a habit of getting in touch with many affected by the loss of someone to see what we can do that it can become a shield for facing our own pain and Grief. The Empress can appear to remind us that we need to love ourselves, the more so at a time such as this.

One of the many things I find myself saying to clients during a reading is that love is the strongest energy there is. I have found that this seems to apply in so many situations, and in so many readings. I often point out that its opposite is fear (not hate as many suppose). In our Grief we can lose touch with this force, in our self, in life and in the Universe.

I have found that a good remedy to this is to focus on loving ourselves. Spoiling ourselves a little when we need to is good therapy. Taking some time out to do something we love can be a good way to connect with the energy of love once again. For me time spent cycling along the seafront for miles near where I live seems to achieve this, as does caring for our garden. Each of the deaths I have experienced in my life has made me more resolute about how short life is and how important it is to use our lives for love. Carpe Diem indeed!

As we move more towards acceptance in our Grief, so we may be able to reflect on the love we shared with our loved one, in whatever way this was. There is something of a move away from traditional funerals these days, to a 'celebration of the life of'. Whilst these can have a role and a place I feel there is still a need for the funeral rite, the celebratory aspect following perhaps. This may be when we begin to feel acceptance of the situation. Then we can reflect, and share in whatever way we might wish, the love both from and to the deceased person. Perhaps then the best celebration can be in the way we continue that love through our own self and life.

I recently said to a fellow Tarot colleague, and I repeat once more, that despite the death of my daughter and my wife's incurable disease, I still have to believe that being alive is a wonderful adventure, that people are still essentially nice and good and the Universe is a benign place. Love is still the strongest energy there is and it always will be. I like to think that this would bring a smile to The Empress' face.

THE EMPEROR

Just as The Empress can epitomize the maternal aspect, so the Emperor can be the paternal. Just like the maternal, this can come in many forms to us, whether physically, or in terms of our own approaches and attitudes. For me, he can exemplify something of what seems to have become a dirty word and concept in recent times, especially in parenting; that of discipline.

Just as we have need for love, care and nurture, so we can also need rules, regulation and yes, discipline. These can be imposed by ourselves or by others, often creating in us an almost instinctive rebellious response. Like all things, they each have their uses and drawbacks. The need for both nurture and rules was always significant for me, symbolised on the card by the river that runs through the background behind The Emperor's throne. This shows he at least acknowledges and actually needs the influence of The Empress. Or we could say that she is the 'power behind the throne'.

The discipline of The Empress can be in her need to learn to address her own needs. For The Emperor it can be the reverse that he needs to be aware of, that of the good of others and the 'greater good'. In this I return to the idea of fear being the opposite of Love. When I look at the Emperor I often wonder what he is fearful of. He seems to make a great bravado, on his throne of solid rock, encased in his full armour and staff of authority. This all brings me to consider what fear he needs to hide behind.

Grief can bring us so closely into touch with our fears. Chief among these may have already been realised of course, with the death of our loved one. Being confronted with death in such a way can bring us to look at our own mortality. One of the many conversations I am glad that I had with Laura concerning Amy's condition was how it had confronted us with our own mortality, and in so doing taken away some of that fear, or at the very least the idea of our trying to ignore or push aside our own death. I like to think that in some way this helped Laura a little.

We may want to think about those things we have fear of in our lives. We can, of course make the requisite list of them. It may be that we do not need or wish to do anything about them, at least while dealing with our Grief fully. It may be that it is enough to acknowledge them, and perhaps consider addressing one or more of them when the time is right. Or we may find it therapeutic at this time to go all out and attack one of our fears, perhaps as a symbolic gesture to honour our loved one.

We might also find that we need a certain amount of the Emperor's discipline, structure and control in our Grief too. I have written before how easy it is for our daily or regular habits and ways to slip in our Grief, and as before, this is fine and understandable in the short term, and can even be useful. At a point however, we need to get back in the metaphorical saddle and return to what we know serves us and our well-being. For me this is a morning routine of brief ritual, yoga and meditation, plus an exercise 'regime' of some kind, cooking my own meals from scratch and so on. All such things require a certain amount of discipline and The Emperor's appearance can help act as a reminder for us, almost like a personal trainer on the sidelines, cheering and urging us on.

More generally, or in summary, I see The Emperor's contribution to our well-being in the idea of control. We each exert a certain amount of control over ourselves and our lives, and we do need some of this in order to be effective in our aspirations and achievements. Yet too much becomes a suppression and unhealthy limitation.

My conclusion can be expressed in one of those delightfully oxymoronic expressions, whereby we achieve the control we need by not controlling. Put another way, we can learn, through the experience and tuition of our Grief, to 'go with the flow', but we must be the creator of that flow. We can learn to respond rather than react to what life presents us with, and in adopting this attitude from within, we can find something akin to the acceptance of this stage of Grief.

THE HIEROPHANT

The Hierophant is a card that I never really liked, in all my years working with the Tarot. I was raised within an atypical Christian belief system, which apart from some of the teachings of Jesus, I never accepted. I think it may have been this that produced my lack of association with this card.

It was only later that I came to see the energy of the card as an expression of what is sacred to each of us, this being an individual thing, in terms of our belief system, and/or relationship with deity or deities. In this The Hierophant reminds me that the purpose of our life is ultimately to learn our own lessons, encased or encoded in our life experiences, and grow from them.

What then, can we learn from Grief? This again, has to be individual. Our Grief can be shaped by the manner and situation of the passing of our loved one, and each one we experience can produce a different aspect of the Grief process. Grief is certainly a reminder that we will die and we do not know when this will be. The death of someone close to us shows us this and we can learn and grow so much from fully accepting it and adjusting our life and lifestyle to take account for it.

This may not only be by way of having a 'carpe diem' attitude, commendable as this might be. It is certainly as if The Hierophant may be exhorting us to really live our life, which for me means a focus on that which is most important and valuable to me and not being drowned in the mediocrity of petty struggles and niggles, whatever they may be. This is how the Hierophant exemplifies what is sacred to us and requires of us to live in accordance with this. In the acceptance of our death we are set free to live our life in such a way that reflects that belief and standing.

It can be easy to think that if we were suddenly diagnosed with a terminal illness we would do all the things we wanted to do, go to the places we wanted to and so on. Yet the reality can be quite different. Having been given exactly this for Amy, the experience we are having, at the time of writing this book, is that we have come to place a greater emphasis on the relationships we have, and on the time we have together. This may be simply spending an evening watching TV together, (and trying not to fall asleep too much), or dragging ourselves out to a local coffee shop. Not exactly memorable and hugely dynamic occurrences perhaps, but to us they are precious and wonderful. We are sharing them and we are together. They are not different to what we did before the diagnosis but we now view and value them differently. This may be part of 'preparatory grief', but it can also be a celebration of our lives. We have both expressed that, although the lifestyle we have now is not what we had planned or could envisage, we still love it and being with the other. In this, it is Sacred for us.

The Hierophant seems to present himself to us as if to ask of our Grief and our loss, 'can you accept this, and still believe'? When The Hierophant appears in your Grief process you may find it helpful to consider this question. What we each believe is up to us, but asking ourselves what we believe in, in terms of a spirituality, or belief system, can help us to connect to the wider world and Universe. Grief can have a way of causing us to turn inward, and sometimes to an unhealthy degree, so here there can be an opportunity to open out again, and re-connect to the idea of a world and Universe 'unfolding as it should'.

It is perhaps when we respond to this question and say 'Yes, this is ok' that we can begin to know acceptance, in our body, heart, mind and soul, of the death and loss we have experienced. Not that it will ever be that we will stop missing them, but we can understand that all things die, and each death has its time and place.

THE LOVERS

As part of 'My Process' – my diary of the 'Tarot Mentoring' process following Laura's death, which is included at the end of this book - I detail how I said to a Tarot colleague that despite Laura's death and Amy's condition, I have to still believe that being alive is a wonderful adventure, the world is an amazing place, people are basically good and that I still believe Love is the strongest energy there is. It may be that the evidence in my recent life would suggest otherwise but this is a choice I make and one which, in my Grief, I need to make. In my worst moments it may feel like this is all I have. This is why I make no bones about continuing to repeat it in this book, it has become something of an affirmation for me.

The Lovers card has been written about as the card of choice. This has always seemed something of a contradiction to me, since it can often seem, or we tell ourselves, that when we fall in love with someone that it is 'destiny', we are 'meant' to be together and we are the requisite 'soul mates'. It is in that first romantic flush of a relationship that we can sense these things and that seems to effectively remove any objective choice we might otherwise make. It can be as if love makes Fools of us, literally, in the Tarot sense!

In Grief, reason can also desert us as we seek to travel through the individual wasteland of our pain, anguish and sorrow. Just as with Love, it can seem that we are being clear-minded but in reality, and to others, we can say and do things that are heavily tainted by our experience and consequent response, as we seek to come to an acceptance of what we have experienced. There is nothing especially wrong with this, and it can be a necessary part of our Grief process, but it can be wise not to come to large and important decisions concerning our lives whilst we are in this phase.

The presence of the Angel in the card, and more commonly in recent decks, Cupid, suggests to me that there is a higher perspective or vantage point possible, and available to us. It may be that we cannot take up this position for a time, but for now it can help us to know it is there. This may take the form of our belief in a higher plan or destiny and we can, at the very least, perhaps take some comfort by telling ourselves that everything is happening as it should do.

For me, this can be in the form of coming to accept and even sense and know within that there are no mistakes in the Universe and the evolution and unfoldment of it all. It is a different matter whether we can see it or not. I have said to a number of people that the older I get, the more Zen I seem to get! By this I mean that I admit and accept that I do not know much, and nor do I need to know much. I know what is right for me, what works for me and what doesn't. I try to live my life as an expression of what I believe and what is sacred to me, and that is enough.

When The Lovers card appears in our Grief process it can be a reminder that we can make choices for ourselves, as well as showing us that we cannot make choices for others, including that of our lost loved one. We could no more control this than we can the direction and strength of the wind or the rain. What use then, in rallying against it, or bemoaning our fate and the cruel nature of the world for the remainder of our days, seeking to express or perhaps free ourselves from the pain we feel. Rather, this card can tell us to acknowledge our pain, to move towards acceptance of the nature of things, and then make a choice to still believe in Love and all that goes with it.

This card is often interpreted as relating to relationships, as well as the overarching experience of Love in our self and life. In our Grief it can be an easy temptation to want to close our hearts off, thereby shielding ourselves from the chances of any further emotional pain and suffering. In so doing we also close ourselves off to the experience of Love as well, in all its varied and wonderful ways and forms. I recall saying to Laura that a response I may well have to Amy's death would be to bury myself alone, in writing and work. She told me that she would not let me. Now that reassurance has been removed I have to make the choice myself. I have many people around me that love me and in this I am fortunate indeed. It is however, only me that can choose to experience that love, both giving and receiving it. I can therefore look forward to the appearance of this card to remind me.

THE CHARIOT

I have always liked this card. It fits my vision of the purpose of life so well, in that it has the energy that propels us onwards and upwards through our life, a force that keeps us going, no matter what. When we are dealing with Grief, this is of course something that can be hugely valuable.

The energy of this card can be the experience we have when everything is going right, things just fall into place and work out as we intend them to. The more I studied and practiced esoteric matters, the more I came to see and experience that we must be the creators of that intention and that flow; it does not 'just happen'. What we put out there is what we experience. In this sense the Universe is like a big mirror, reflecting back to us what we project from within in the form of what we experience and what 'happens' to us.

As I came to know and relate more to this card I saw in it a theme of alignment and unity. This is an alignment with our own individual, or human will with that of a higher or if you prefer, divine will. It is the unity depicted in the card of the charioteer with the horses that pull everything along. It is the blend of forces and energies that coalesce when we tune into our inner senses and flow into and with what we sense and know are the right things to do in our life. Gandhi is often (and 'mis') quoted as saying 'Be the change you wish to see in the world'. With apologies to the Mahatma I can offer this, here adjusted to 'Be the Focus you wish to experience in the world'.

The acceptance in this card I think can be a difficult one to allow. This is because that it can be natural to think that we did not focus on the death of our loved one, and nor may have they, but it still happened. In this I turn to my previous statement about 'becoming more Zen' and the admittance that we do not and cannot know why anyone died when and how they did, but they did. Laura certainly did not place a focus on her death but it happened one Sunday morning as she drank a cup of coffee, nothing more than that. So why did it happen? Because it did.

Acceptance here can only be in accepting the fact, and quite possibly without knowing the reason. It is then that we can begin to experience the unity of our own will with something greater than that. In doing so my experience is that there is a peace that comes with it. It is truly a 'peace that passes all understanding' since there is absolutely no reason to do so. But the alternative is to place ourselves in opposition to the natural way of things and this never ends well.

It is then a choice between what or who is at the centre of our world and the Universe we inhabit. We may indeed create our own reality and be the chief architect of it, but this does not mean that we are at the centre of everything and that it all revolves or evolves around us. Rather it is a symbiotic relationship and the energy of this card, the smooth flow of natural progression and 'effortless effort', is what we can experience when we allow ourselves to accept this.

It is often said that this card is about our will, and our willpower. It can be said that when The Chariot appears it is telling us we need to exert our strength of will and 'keep on keeping on'. There is a difference between will power and being willful however. We have great resources within our will that can truly create wondrous and magical things as history can show us, but we cannot and will not get it right all the time, succeed every time and force things to happen the way we want them to every time. Sometimes things work, sometimes they do not.

This can be abundantly clear when we are experiencing Grief and the key to the energy of this card can come from a simple and largely unquestioning acceptance of this.

STRENGTH

It is common to point out that this card does not relate to physical Strength, but instead a force within, something that is more of a quality of character than muscle development. It is also not to be associated with inner will, which as we have seen lies more properly with the previous card.

Often subtitled 'The Lady and The Lion', the card shows the lady in question with one hand above and one below the lions open jaw. They are in most cases, gazing into each other's eyes, which can suggest some kind of hypnotic effect. It is significant that above the lady floats the lemniscate, the symbol for infinity, which seems to have become almost ubiquitous these days!

There could be a number of words used to describe the quality that the energy of this card seeks to connect us with: self-control, resilience, tenacity, perseverance, as well as fortitude and courage, these last two being alternative names for the card.

It is easy to say that these are all qualities we need and can benefit from whilst we process our Grief. The contradiction or paradox here can be that these are just the things that are hard for us to feel or sense, lacking the necessary, well, strength, to do so. When in Grief it can be a huge, all-consuming effort to get out of bed and face the day, let alone cook a nutritious meal for ourselves or contemplate meeting anyone. Our Grief can be the only thing we are aware of and may want to be concerned with.

To help us with this conundrum we can look a little further at the image. Doing what the lady is would seem a foolish thing to do, but she shows no fear, and the lion for his part seems happy enough with the process. From this I see that rather than letting what might seem to be an enemy threaten our well-being or even survival, we can gain much from the acceptance of this position and doing what we can best do in it.

Our Grief is what it is and it certainly seems and feels to us that we are the only ones that knows just what it is like. Our relationship with our loved one who has died was unique after all, so this is true in one respect. Given that this is the case, it follows that it may only be us that knows how to best respond to it and come to deal with it. As we see repeatedly with these Major Arcana cards, this can have to do with acceptance.

We know the pain of our Grief, and everything else associated with it. By accepting this within ourselves, we can begin to gain some dominion over it. In so doing we can begin to change our view of the lion that threatens in its roar to devour us to an ally, to show and offer us power and grace.

The acceptance I am referring to here is an inner thing, just like the qualities it can then give rise to, as listed above at the start of this card's musings. With regard to how to move to this acceptance, my sense, based on what I have learnt to do and apply, pretty much daily since Laura's death, is to make a choice to apply compassion to myself, to love myself enough to do this. This can be to take the time I need to address my needs, in my case beginning my day with a time of yoga, meditation and greeting the Elements and powers that populate my Universe. I drink hot water with lemon, then a cup of Earl Grey tea, and read for a time. Occasionally I do none of these and just lounge in bed with my tea for a time watching the TV. Either way, I am accepting myself and responding to this with my choice of how I start my day.

This is my application of the Strength card and one that each day gives me greater resolve to get through the day and also to make progress with it, with myself, those around me and the wider Universe. It is these things that are the motivation for me I now have, given the situation life has given me. Sometimes the progress I make is to choose to not do very much because I need to allow some time to be sad and do whatever I need to as a result. When these days happen I now remind myself that I hope to feel different the following morning, and when I check in with myself, I invariably do. If I don't then it is time for a little (or large) lion roar and determination and resilience to be applied. I make sure, or even force myself, to do some yoga and the flow of energy through my body – physical and energetic– gets things moving on all levels. I can then let out a different kind of roar!

THE HERMIT

I think that The Hermit can be a much maligned figure in the Tarot, since many people who are not familiar or knowledgeable with the it and some who are, see him as a lonely old man living out his days alone, wandering aimlessly about in the dark, able only to see as far as the light from his lamp reaches. In the last card we saw the power and strength that can come from making our own choices, and it is vital to realise that The Hermit is where and how he is by his own choosing and design.

Here he stands, in what for him is 'splendid isolation'. He does not need the company of others, but is happy to show them the way to his position if they wish to come. He has chosen the 'road less travelled' and this is where it has taken him. He may have more years behind him than there are ahead, but he is content with everything as it is and requires nothing more. He has rejected the way of the herd and his life is his own.

In Grief, we can begin our approach to coming to know the Hermit by seeing the difference between loneliness and being alone. These are both subjects that can be paramount for us in the aftermath of a loved one dying, particularly if that person was a partner, and we are now living alone as a result. So many times I have had Tarot clients ask for a reading about their relationship where it becomes clear they are thinking of ending the one they are in. Very often they say they have not done so either because they do not want to be alone, or they do not want to hurt their partner.

To the former I ask them to consider which may be worse, years of being at best less than satisfied or some time spent alone where they can be free to start anew. To the latter I suggest considering which hurts them more, leaving them now or keeping hold of them when you know you are not giving them the love they deserve (and themselves of course). It is so often the case that they know these things but feel that they needed 'permission'. This permission they can only give to themselves. The Tarot can show them this in a gentle yet effective manner.

Of course in Grief we do not choose to be alone, and this is a big difference. It's onset was out of our control and there was ultimately nothing we could do to stop it. We can however, have at least some control over how we respond. When The Hermit appears for us, it may be that he is asking us to look to our 'aloneness', whether this is physical or otherwise; to that part of us that is now without the presence of our loved one. It is as if he asks us 'What do you sense in that space and how might you wish to respond to it'?

It can be important to see here that it is not about just 'filling' that space, putting something into ourselves or lives as a replacement – how can there ever be a replacement for our loved one? There can though, be an adjustment. The exact nature of that adjustment will depend to some degree on our individual situation. However, it becomes clear that The Hermit can be offering us, in the acceptance of our new situation, a different way to what went before and one in which there is a new freedom, despite the separation and loss.

I see in the Hermit one who has, perhaps long ago, shifted from any sense of co-dependency in his relationships. This is something that is again common to see in Tarot clients that come to me. One of the most common traits is that they end one relationship, start another and in so doing find a repeating pattern. So often the cards they choose show them a need to not be in a relationship, or in a relationship with themselves; a chance to learn to love themselves first. Perhaps in the acceptance of this possibility in our Grief we can shift from being focused on loss and loneliness to learning and love.

This is the beginning of the wisdom in life that The Hermit has acquired and he is pleased to offer this to all of us that care to come to him.

THE WHEEL OF FORTUNE

One of the aspects of the Major Arana cards I try to get across to Tarot students is that the energy they portray is bigger and stronger, and very often more far-reaching, than we individual human beings are. Their effect can reach every level of our being and that of the whole self, identified holistically as being 'greater than the sum of the parts'. Arguably, this is most easily seen in this card.

The general message can be summarized in the gravitational adage 'what goes up, must come down', applied to our fortunes as we live our lives. There are several such phrases that can be applied here, such as the Biblical 'to everything there is a season' and the comforting 'this too shall pass'. Perhaps the energy of this card can be best surmised for our purposes here as Romeo's declaration that 'I am fortune's Fool'.

This is certainly how we might feel when dealing with the loss of a loved one from our lives. There is in this the stark reminder that we cannot control such things and yet are affected by them to an almost equally uncontrollable degree. My sense is to respond to this fact by considering that it is then pointless and useless to rally against it, and either adopt an ongoing attitude in life of anger or resentment which is likely to evolve into a bitterness that saps the life out of anyone. To my mind it is better to recognise that greater forces exist in our lives and whilst we can play a full part in shaping them, there is a level beyond us. Better then to come to terms with and find acceptance of this.

This does not mean that we should just be acquiescent in our life. We choose whether we turn left or right at every junction and the Wheel turns just the same. When I look at this card I am sometimes reminded of the circus 'knife-throwing act' where the hapless subject is tied to a wheel that is spun and the (sometimes blindfolded) knife thrower does his worst. This principle is all so aptly and wonderfully put in Shakespeare's 'To be or not to be' speech (Hamlet Act 111 Scene 1. Do read it, you can understand what this card is about so much more poetically, as we seek to dodge 'the slings and arrows of outrageous fortune'.

This being the case my thought is often to consider where we are upon the Wheel when the card appears for us. Most certainly in Grief we can be on the rim, spinning ceaselessly and wildly, trying to make our way through each day like a child who has just stepped off the playground roundabout and whose legs will not hold them up. My suggestion is to consider what is needed to bring us to the centre of the Wheel. There the spinning is felt less, yet everything still continues and evolves just as it should.

For me the centre of the Wheel is also the centre of ourselves. It is always there, and nothing that we do or that happens to us can remove or displace it. To find it, I have found it is necessary only to sit and breathe. Nothing more than that. As we close our eyes, let ourselves be physically comfortable and bring our breath to below the diaphragm, so we receive more oxygen with each breath and the mind too can breathe a little more. By just doing this for several minutes (or however long, or short, a time it takes) we gain a sense of calm and even stillness, despite the continued turning of the Wheel.

I also see in this card a reminder to be gentle, forgiving and compassionate to ourselves in our Grief. The nature of things is such that we cannot get it right all the time, we cannot be 'up' or positive all the time and we are allowed to be down and to be negative on occasion. The trick is to avoid getting stuck in either of these phases, but instead to learn to go actively with the flow, of our lives, and with our Grief. When we are understanding of this we can allow ourselves and accept the days and times when we apparently are not 'getting it right'. We know that the Wheel will turn once more, but the peace can remain. In this way we can experience more of the constant that lies at the centre of the Wheel.

JUSTICE

For me the chief assets of the Justice card are truth and honesty. Seated at the centre of the journey through the Major Arcana I have often said that this is where we meet ourselves coming back the other way! In other words this is where we see and face ourselves exactly as we really and truly are, rather than some imagined ideal or view that we have told ourselves is who and what we are. If we are able to do this and reach a place of true acceptance of what we come across, then we can gain a real sense of self-worth and understanding that is truly powerful in life.

The root of this power I see as coming from love of self. I also think this is one of the toughest nuts to crack on our quest. To love ourselves as we are requires of us that we look wide-eyed and with clarity at all that we have done before, and in the understanding we have now, forgive ourselves for whatever we did that causes our conscience disquiet. In all honesty it took me until my mid 40's before I felt I loved myself as I should. Not because I had done so many bad things or could not forgive myself, but because I was aware of there being things I simply either did not like about myself or knew I still needed to work on. It was only when I came to see that I could love myself just as I was, and not despite but because of my faults, that I had indeed 'cracked it'. I came to love myself simply because I am, nothing more and nothing less.

Along the way I found I had to look at the links between the things I had done in my life and the consequences those things had. This is of course ongoing. The energy of this card presents us with a direct connection between the inner and the outer, between thought and deed, action and consequence. In doing so we have to take responsibility for all that we are.

Amidst all of this process there is a connection and sometimes a confrontation with the major times and events in our lives, those pivotal moments that can shape the direction of our lives and our character. The experience of the death of a loved one is most certainly one of these.

The appearance of this card may be bringing you to a time when there is a need to look at yourself and your life in the light of this new reality. In the aftermath of the death you have experienced who are you now and what is your life now? These are difficult questions and there may not be answers so much as responses to them, in all different kinds of ways. Be mindful of the things that come to you immediately, whether they be thoughts, feelings, images or anything at all. Note these and refer back to them after some time has elapsed. It may be then that the answers come to you.

I also repeat here the necessity and the power of loving the self, and suggest that this can be the acceptance encoded in the energy of this card that helps us navigate our way through our Grief. Justice always requires of us total honesty and truth, but we can be rewarded with a love for the self that arises from this acceptance.

Any counsellor will tell you that their job is not to give you answers, or tell you what they think or what to do. Much of their task can be to hear and to validate what you say. This can of course be a very valuable part of our Grief process that some may choose. For me, the Tarot became my counsellor(s). As can be seen in 'My Process' at the end of the book, the Tarot gave me answers or responses when I had questions about my Grief, and when I had none gave me guidance and suggestions. Both of course have their place and value.

THE HANGED MAN

This card seems to aptly sum up the principle that what we see on the outside may not be what is happening on the inside, when we observe any other person. We see the figure on the card hanging upside down, usually tethered to a tree by one ankle. In the short term, being inverted can have many positive effects, as any yoga practitioner will tell you. The opposite is true for a prolonged period of time however.

The card often points towards an inner transformation, rather than an outer one, and this may be the case as we learn to traverse the landscape of our Grief, inwardly and outwardly. The outer situation we may be experiencing following the death of a loved one can of course be something we did not ask for, was out of our control and so something we simply have come to learn to accept. The move to the acceptance that is required needs to happen first on the inside.

This is shown in the oft-referred to analyses of this card in the Hanged Man's expression of peace, along with the halo or aura that surrounds his head. This can be taken as the effect of the head-stand pose of yoga as the life-force flows there as a result, but can also be seen in the inner poise, or even mastery, adopted by the Hanged Man in the situation he finds himself in.

This is neither resignation nor acquiescence. Whilst our emotions in Grief may make it easy to assume both these traits, we really need to guard against adopting or becoming used to such a stance, since we can be led towards apathy that can give rise to laziness and a depressive, 'laissez-faire' attitude that removes a sense of power or active participation in our life and its unfoldment from here on. I am pleased to say that I have thus far avoided inclusion of the somewhat clichéd question 'is that what *insert name of loved one* would want', but here it seems entirely, and slightly annoyingly, appropriate.

I have mentioned before that one of the chief and most powerful lessons I have learned from the deaths I have experienced, and most prominent of all these being Laura's, not because of its recentness but because of her age and situation, is to approach my life knowing that I do not know how long it will last, and so to make the most of who and what I have got in it. If that is not what I would wish, then I do all I can to change and create it, to find what I do want. This is not done from a negative point of view, but from a standpoint of life as a positive celebration and still an exciting adventure.

The acceptance of this card is first an inner thing as we have seen, and an active thing which needs to take place at our core. When we consider the Hanged Man being tied from one ankle, we can see that with an exerted effort, and a good deal of core strength, he could lever himself up and untie his bonds. With a little more control he can make a landing so as not to injure himself, get up, dust himself off and continue on his way. This can be analogous to our Grief process, only not in any flippant a manner as I have made it sound.

It boils down to the perspective we can choose to take of our situation. We may choose to be resentful, or allow the sadness of our situation to colour and shape our self and life from here on. Equally we can, if necessary to start with, force ourselves to accept things as they are and resolve to become active in our self and life because of our Grief, thereby beginning a process that can bring us to being at peace with it. How we do this is a matter for each one of us, but it is what the Hanged Man can show us when he appears. For me, it can be with a hug, whether from someone else, or myself. This simple, yet so expressive an act can be a visceral reminder that all will be, and indeed, is, well.

DEATH

There can obviously be something of an irony when this card appears in our Grief process and we may want to emit a snort of derision when it does so. We may instantly think along the lines of 'what can this card show me I don't already know' and we can forgive ourselves for this reaction. Our thoughts and feelings are no doubt full of the subject of death and all that goes with it, so it can seem as if this is either superfluous or insulting.

Death is part of the human experience and as such it can represent an initiation, both for those who have undergone the transformation of it and those of us 'left behind' who are the ones that can suffer. In her own Grief following Laura's death, Amy would wonder many times how Laura was and I tried my best each time to reassure her that Laura is now absolutely fine, and that it was Amy's natural inclination to worry about her. Amy knew this anyway, but in Grief the logical and natural workings of the mind can get twisted.

Whilst a funeral can be a collective ritual that plays a vital part, again both for the deceased and their loved ones in the initiation process, there can also be a place for your own, more private ceremony you may wish to engage in. This can take many forms, from a visit to a shared place in the loved one's honour, purchase of a candle to burn each year on their birthday, recitation of your own words to them, to a full magical rite to give thanks. Whatever your chosen act, this can be a powerful way to mark a shift, both for them and in your own self and life.

Any initiation is in part a transformative shift, an acknowledgement of a stage reached and an adjustment to it. The experience of the death of a loved one certainly fulfils this criteria and in some ways our lives and our selves may never be the same after it. This is said to imply neither a negative nor positive, it is simply a recognition of the shift. It is something we cannot deny, much as we might like to, and the appearance of this card may be showing you a need to come to an acceptance of this change.

It is hard to be in a state of denial when something so real as the death of a loved one has happened, but as we have already seen, this is one of the recognized stages of the Grief process. It is not so much a denial that it has happened as an apparent inability to take it in. It is only within ourselves that we can effect the shift into acceptance and my sense is that when this card appears it is a reminder, suggestion or even a challenge to us to strive to reach this stage.

You may know of the Major Arcana being equated with the Hero's Journey, the mythological process of transformation and initiation, effectively from innocence to maturity. It is common for the invitation to this journey to be refused or denied initially, then to be accepted when offered again. So in the stark reality of the energy of this card we can have compassion for ourselves if we are not yet ready or able to make that shift. It can be enough to recognize it and say 'no, not yet'. It is only when we are ready that we can embrace it, and the initiatory transformation, both within and without, takes root.

TEMPERANCE

After the sometimes not easy shifts and transformation of previous cards, the appearance of the 'Angel of Temperance' can seem to be a welcome one. With a foot in both worlds, the Angel can be seen as creating a different kind of change, as they pour the 'water of life' from one cup to the other, the alchemy of the process blending above with below, within with without and acting as a bridge between the worlds.

That bridge can certainly be a welcome one to behold, in whatever way we may do so, in our Grief. The concept of the 'Rainbow Bridge' as it is known, has been a feature in the Western Mysteries and Theosophy, and is analogous to our journey to a sense of unity with the Soul, and the inner work we do to build a 'bridge between the worlds'. This card can in effect, offer us the energy to do this in our Grief.

Talking to the dead has been something not uncommon in our house, ever since Amy and I got together! That has not changed following Laura's death, albeit with a different type of feeling to it. Whether we engage in any type of communication with our deceased loved one is a personal choice of course, but the point being made here is that it can be a perfectly normal thing when one takes into account a view of death such as we have.

This is principally that there is no death, only the function of the physical body stops, thereby releasing the portion of the Soul that inhabited it. This then lives in its own realm, whether we call this the Otherworld, Spirit world, Heaven or whatever. This being the case, why should we not then communicate with them? This does not require any special attitude or reverence and can be done just as with a normal conversation. Replies, if any, may be different of course, and again, this can be an individual thing and depend to a large degree on the means by which we believe or think this might happen.

Either way, when this card appears, it can be good to consider if in your Grief you wish or need to communicate with your loved one. You might like to write them a letter, sit and talk to them, write a poem or paint a picture for them. This can be an entirely therapeutic thing apart from any other aspect related to it, and can bring healing that this card is often associated with, here in the form of an acceptance that our loved one may have physically died but is not lost to us.

I have written much about transformation in the preceding cards and this process can be seen as continuing through the energy of this card too. This can be from the effect of the acceptance it can bring, as described above. It has been my experience that I have been transformed by the deaths I have experienced through my life, each one adding something to the present reality of my life, of the person that I am and how I inhabit that life. It can be hard to pinpoint or put into words exactly what and how that transformation has occurred or taken effect, but chief among those has certainly been the value that I now place on life and every part of it. I value the people in my life so much more now than ever before and I think I am very fortunate to know so many lovely ones. I live my life not so much with a sense of urgency because I know it is, or can be, so brief, but from a place of wanting to achieve as much as I can, grow as much as I can and give as much as I can, not necessarily in that order!

For me this is the Peace that this Angel brings when I see them, and a reassurance that actually, however I might feel in this moment of my Grief, everything is ok. Any tears I might cry are then ultimately healing, and this brings me to the acceptance within that I need.

THE DEVIL

When this card appears I often explain that far from being something the client need fear, The Devil can actually be our best friend. He is after all, derived from Lucifer, the 'Bringer of Light'. In the Tarot the card is usually seen as that which seeks to repress us, restrict us and hold us back. The Devil can cause us to behave with compulsion or obsession, hence the associations with avarice and addiction. This can give rise to lies and dishonesty.

If we look a little further from this catalogue of oppression we can see that these are all things we need to rid ourselves of and be free from. It is in this way that the energy of The Devil serves to highlight those things that are holding us back, precisely because of our need for freedom from them. The more we are restricted the more we can feel the need to escape and push beyond those limits and whatever chains us to our respective blocks. This is the gift of The Devil.

It is commonly noted that the chains around the necks of the male and female figures in the card are large enough for them to remove themselves. This tells us that the power rests not as we may think, with The Devil, but with us. For me it is as if he is there, doing his best to look intimidating or frightening to say 'Look, you believe I have got you by the short and curlies, but you are letting me. What are you going to do about it'?

In terms of Grief, when this card appears in our process, it can be that we need to take a look at what seems to be holding us back now. This is not our Grief itself or the sadness that we will feel at times which we are absolutely allowed and need to. We also need to release them, oppression only coming into this equation when we do not, or feel we should or cannot, voice or express what we have within. The appearance of this card can be a herald to look into ourselves and see what, if any, dark, compulsive and perhaps illogical and obsessive thoughts we might be having. This for me is an all too apparent need, since Laura and I agreed to share such things following Amy's diagnosis, which we did, so now I do not have that valve to open. In the aftermath of the death of your loved one it might be that your inner self has silently and subtly taken on board some limiting or 'negative' beliefs that are sharing or colouring your view of the world, and thereby your life and the way you live it. In this case, The Devil may be showing you that it is time to forgive yourself if this if necessary, apply some self-love and do what is needed to shift from this state.

The history of humanity is, unfortunately, such that we very often learn what is right by doing what is wrong. This can be true on an international, national, community, family and individual level. In Tarot terms it is The Devil card that does this, because by highlighting how not to do things we can learn how to do them successfully. The danger in this can come when we become stuck in a morass of helplessness and apathy, believing the lie that there is no point in trying anymore because 'life's a bitch and then you die'. This is all illustrated by Thomas Edison, who when asked how it felt to have been unable to get any results in trying to create a lightbulb said *"Results! Why, man, I have gotten a lot of results! I know several thousand things that won't work."*

Is there a successful way to do Grief? Certainly, it is your way. What can be required here is to consider what this is, what we may have allowed to prevent us from doing this, then to accept these things and respond actively to them with the intention of bringing light to ourselves and our lives, so as to be free from restriction. In this sense The Devil shows us how to grieve properly and fully.

THE TOWER

This is another of the cards that when we are in Grief we can immediately identify with, our world seeming and feeing like it has all come crashing down around us. This we know, and only too well, so we need to consider what this card can show us beyond this scenario of 'stating the obvious'.

As with all Major Arcana cards we are concerned with forces and energies that are bigger and stronger than we are and that therefore impact the whole of our being, or put another way, affect us at a Soul level. In the energy of this card we are or have been subject to the destruction and removal of that which we thought was secure, or that we placed our security in and believed was permanent. The energy here is a graphic and immediate demonstration that nothing is permanent in our life, as we have experienced with the death of our loved one.

Avoiding the truism that the only permanence is impermanence, when this card appears its energy can serve to show us that whatever attempts we may have made to place security in, structures built and relationships made, all are subject to change and to destruction and removal. The energy here is the loss of what was familiar and known, and about which we could do nothing, as with the death of someone we love. The card can show us therefore that we can place our security only in the knowledge and the inner acceptance, that there is none.

Problems can tend to occur when we have used the Tower as a hiding place, a place of refuge in which we seek to either deny the forces of change or convince ourselves that they have not happened or affected us in anyway. The Tower can maintain the status quo and keep us comfortable and safe. Except that it cannot. Whatever we seek to hold back or down must eventually erupt, from even the tiniest fissure that it will find.

The energy and experience of this card is like the volcano that must erupt. It is the natural conclusion and consequence of the pressure from beneath and within. We can however choose to see this as the means by which the light and power within comes to the fore, and creates a new structure and reality. The guidance of the Tower can be to let your light shine, not hide it away. With reference to Grief this is about acceptance of our new reality following the death. This can take time of course, but we cannot and should not deny who we are as a consequence of what our life now is. Put more poetically and in sublime tones by the great Leonard Cohen: 'There is a crack in everything, that's how the light gets in'.

The experience of the Tower card can be something of a stark confrontation and a difficult one to navigate, but is ultimately healing. It can feel as if the Tower represents the sum total of our anxieties and fears and in one stormy night we are exposed in our Grief. Yet we can find that this seemingly very worst of things need not reduce us or make us less than we were before. Different yes, but not less.

The gift that the destruction of our Tower brings us is that we can live from this point knowing that our fears are not insurmountable, the cause of our anxieties is not unbeatable and we have something within us that even in death will always find a way to shine. We can say to our Tower, like Obi-Wan Kenobi facing Darth Vader: 'Strike me down and I shall become more powerful than you can possibly imagine'.

THE STAR

It is often said that this card is all about Hope. Every time I see or hear this I am reminded of a discussion I had with my first meditation teacher about Hope and Pandora's Box. The story is that Pandora's curiosity led her to open a box (actually a jar) left in the care of her husband. Opening it released physical and emotional curses onto mankind, sometimes said as letting evil or all of humanity's ills into the world. When it was emptied, the only thing left was Hope. The question our discussion focused on was whether Hope is thus a good or bad thing.

In truth it can be both. It can help motivate and encourage us to go after our goals, but if it is all we have we can be doomed to an endless Quest that never gives fulfilment. In Grief there can seem to be little, if any hope. For our loved one the only hope we can have for them is that they have gone to 'a better place' of whatever concept we hold to and we can offer ourselves some comfort from this. As I have mentioned before it is for those of us still here that the hard part remains. We have to find something to hope for in the world and our self following the devastating loss of this person from our life.

When we reflect on the nature of a Star, we know that they are a very long way away – light years in fact. The light from the nearest Star to Earth (The Sun) takes over eight minutes to reach us. The Firmament of the night sky is beautiful, but distant. Yet to see it, we must look up, raising our gaze to focus on something so distant, yet that we can still relate to. The science of astrology shows us something of the energy and connection we have with the Stars and the symbiotic relationship we have with the Universe. For me, this reminds me that the only death we have is that of the physical part of us, but 'we', the identity and energy of who we are, still exists. This tells me that all is not lost, I am not lost, and I am still connected to my loved one, and to the meaning and purpose of my life. This renews hope, restores faith and this sense, thought and then feeling works its way out as motivation to act, to continue not as I was before but different, changed, and valuing everything that bit more because of this. In this way, the Stars are not distant, they are within me, as is my Hope.

There are usually seven Stars on this card, a reference that can be applied to seven being the numerical vibration of the Earth plane of our existence - there being seven notes in the musical scale, seven days of our week and most importantly, seven chakras in our energy body system, along with seven layers to our auric field. This brings to mind the Hermetic adage of 'As Above, So Below' and is another reminder of that intrinsic connection we have with all things - 'As Within, So Without'. In this I find something of a reassurance that, despite my suffering, pain and sadness, it is but a tiny drop in a vast field of energy - hugely significant to me, but there is a bigger perspective. There is a reminder and comfort knowing this, that despite my loved one's death, everything is just as it should be.

This is what I see when I look at the lady of this card. She seems not to consider or care where the water she pours from one of the jars goes to. Her focus is on the one she pours into the pool of water. Yet both have their place, their function and their value, and again, go where they are supposed to go; all is as it should be. This tells me that even though it can feel like it now and at certain times in my life, and in certain parts of myself, I am never alone, the Universe is with me, is part of me, and therefore my Grief. It reaches out to me as I mourn and tells me all is ok.

THE MOON

Ever since I was a child I have had a fascination with the Moon, perhaps stemming from sleeping with my bedroom curtains open so its light would shine on me. Perhaps it's no surprise my career has revolved around the Tarot one way and another! I did not plan this however, I have only followed the inner promptings that felt right to me, in what I was doing with the Tarot, and thus far it has brought me here.

This is very much in keeping with the nature and influence of this card, and the energy we receive from The Moon. It is a subtle and an inner one, and not one that we can discern or work out by logic or calculation. Rather, it speaks to us via our intuitive sense and by shining its light into the darker recesses of our soul, and in my experience, especially so when we are deep in that darkness, which of course we are in Grief.

For me, the Tarot seems to have a way of not shying away from the deepest and darkest corners of our body, heart, mind and soul. In many ways, it actually seems to prefer these places, since this is where it can be of most use and guide us (back) towards the light of our being and the Universe. The experience and process of Grief can most certainly be a very dark one, partly because in the main it is individual, in the private, inner sense of the word. No-one can do it for us, or explain it. It simply is. Some days it is bigger than others, some days the darkness greater. It fluctuates and changes, just as the Moon waxes and wanes.

This is where and how the energy of this card can help us when it appears. It can act first as a simple reminder that all things pass, and that the way we might feel now, will not be how we feel the next day. It tells us that all things have their time and their season, which includes the life and death of our loved one, of all those we love, and ourselves. It tells us that all things happen as they should and at the right time, for them. We may or may not be party to the underlying cause or reason for this and may not be able to have the bigger and higher perspective that the Moon has from her vantage point and so can lack sight of this.

When we look at the image on the card we can see that there is a path ahead, shrouded in shady moonlight as it may yet be. It reminds me of Robert Frosts' 'road less travelled' and seems to beckon us onwards and upwards. Its destination may be out of sight, as can much under the light of the Moon but if we look within, we can sense and come to know within us that there is one. This alone can provide a great comfort as well as motivation as we process our Grief.

More traditionally this card is said to bring about confusion and sometimes a mental strain. The subject of mental health has now become a huge thing in our media and this card can act as a summary of all that goes with this. In Grief it can be enough to get through one day and then the next, for a time at least, let alone consider our state of mind. In the throes of the loss of our loved one, confusion, fear, questions and so on can be the chief residents in our mind. The Moon appears to us as if to tell us that this is ok, they are but temporary lodgers, or even squatters and we can and will evict them when the time is right. If we look within, past the tumult and turmoil we can find a place that, despite all this, is quiet and knows.

This place knows that the state of our not knowing what day it is, which way is up, what we will do without our loved one, how life will ever be the same again and the myriad thoughts in front of it, actually allows for the knowing that lives in a place deeper in our being, and in the Universe too, to gently and gradually rise and fall, and when the time is right, we notice it, sense it and embrace it. We can call this acceptance.

THE SUN

It is common in readings for clients (and some readers too) to want to shy away from the harder cards, those that look like they mean something horrible or unpleasant. Those of you who know my other work on the Tarot know that this is a position I do not take, if anything actually diving right into those harder or darker cards, because these are often the times and places when we can learn and grow the most.

The writing of this book has seen the opposite to this principle apply. It has actually been the brighter, more apparently hopeful, positive ones, such as The Sun of course, that can be harder to relate to when it comes to Grief. Perhaps the most immediate, strongest or most powerful emotion we feel in Grief is sadness and so when a card such as this appears, our first response can be to want to dismiss it since we know very well that we do not feel happiness, optimism, freedom and all the bountiful and beautiful things it is apparently bringing us.

As we know, Grief is not a logical process. There can be something of an unspoken pressure not to be happy, and guilt can ensue when we realise that we have been light in our mood or demeanor for a while. To begin with our loved one is in our thoughts all the time and as the days drift by, little by little, there are minutes and then even an hour, when we do not think about them, or they are at least not the most prominent thing. Then we get reminded in some way and it drags us down to the bottom of the pit of sadness again.

It can sometimes seem that everywhere we turn there are those reminders, of death and of our loved one. It is just like this when you or a family member either is or might be pregnant - babies and pregnant people are everywhere! The evening before I write this, Amy and I were searching for something to watch on TV and Amy suggested we find a 'feel-good' film. We found a comedy that had us both chuckling away, then half way through one character got diagnosed with cancer, and her daughter's name was Laura! There is something of a divine irony in the Universe at times.

The appearance of this card can be a reminder of a different kind. It can tell us that the world out there is still a wonderful one and there are people across it who are experiencing happiness in all kinds of different ways. It may feel like they are in a separate place to us just now, encased as we are in our Grief, symbolized by the garden wall in the card, but then exposure to the full glare of the Sun is not a good thing these days, lest we burn. This card can tell us that the Sun is still there, no matter how big, dark, heavy and complete the cloud cover may be for us. Above them, it is there, sustaining life and creating growth. When I see this card it is for me like the lift we feel within when the Sun does 'come out' – at least for those of us living in England anyway!

For me the appearance of this card is like being given permission to live my life, and even to enjoy it. Not despite my grief but with it. It does not tell me that I can 'beat' my Grief and still be happy. It tells me that my Grief is part of life and as such there is still happiness to be experienced as well as sadness, it is ok to play, feel freedom and enjoy the pleasures of life that I choose to have. We can see this card as a message or instruction from our loved one to not just keep going, but actually to really live our life.

I have mentioned before that the Grief I have experienced, and most of all from witnessing Laura's death, has shown me most of all that life can be so very short and that it is what we make of it while we are here, the relationships we have with people and how we treat others that matters. In the body we have we get one crack at it and no-one can do It for us. The appearance of this card gives me the energy lift needed sometimes to pull me out of the mire and remember that life is there, no matter what, and that I want mine to matter.

JUDGEMENT

As we relate this card to our experience of Grief the idea of the resurrection it depicts may not be far away from our consciousness. We can see in this a comforting message that the soul of our loved one lives on and they have moved to a realm that is not physical, in whatever way we might conceive of this.

For me this card has been much like The Hierophant in that its biblical imagery sits at odds with what I get from it energetically. Rather than the dead being raised at the trumpet call of the Angel on the day of judgement or atonement, I see in this card a call to be the best version of ourselves that we can be, an invitation to 'rise and shine', to lift ourselves up from the daily drudge of mediocrity, whatever that is for each of us, and live a life of purpose, meaning and fulfilment.

In this call and invitation the energy and experience of this card can be likened again to the call to adventure that heralds the start of the quest of the 'Hero's Journey', described so well and eloquently by Joseph Campbell and which forms the basis or perception of so many stories, tales and films. That Quest is often refused at first and in our Grief we can certainly feel as if we do not wish for an adventure, or stimulus of any kind in fact. We may find ourselves not wanting to face the rest of our lives and if we do it can seem a bleak prospect.

It is all too easy to say 'just do it', whatever the marketing might tell us. In Grief we have to fight for the motivation, the focus, the energy and just the breath of will to not let it consume us. There have been several people that have said to me that they do not know what they would do if they lost their child, how they would cope and that they would not survive. I say to them that they would, because they have to.

Once that basic choice is made we come to Andy Dufrane's maxim in the evergreen 'Shawshank Redemption' film that we have 'a simple choice. To get busy living or get busy dying'. To locate and start the engine of the motivation to do this, we might like to make two lists on either side of a sheet of paper, one each for being busy dying, one for being busy living. We can take the various aspects of what we are doing now and what we would like to do and place them under each heading as appropriate – the different things at different levels that we feel contribute overall to each. This show us the things we need to work on not doing and what we need to focus on beginning, continuing or increasing instead.

It is then that the call to journey is presented again. We can choose to see the call as coming from our loved one 'from the other side', inviting and beckoning us on and use our Grief as a springboard over a life of Thoreau's 'quiet desperation'. When the Judgement card appears I see it as a message telling me 'you got this', to use a trendy phrase; that I can get over whatever obstacles I may be facing, exceed my expectations and in this situation, make my loved one not just proud, but marvel at what I do.

This for me, is the resurrection of this card. Ironically enough, I have found that it is the writing of this book that has been my version of getting busy living. I also know that when it is complete I need to focus on another book, or another project. This is not because of any avoidance of facing the pain of my Grief, but because in its acceptance it is my way of responding to the experience and what I have learned, even gained, from it. In this I honour Laura and her life and love. That is why this book is dedicated to her.

THE WORLD

It is widely assumed that when this card appears it heralds a time of victory, the culmination of projects ending in success and in general, everyone living happily ever after! My somewhat caustic tone here is deliberate since in Grief, it is highly unlikely we can see victory in anything, let alone a concept of living happily.

When I look at this image I see the four Elements, however they might be symbolised in the deck, with the central figure acting as the unity of these. For me, this is when everything comes together and the energy of this card is the full experience of everything coming together, and we experience the full force of life, whatever this is for us at the time and however each one of us needs to experience it.

In Grief, it is another reminder from the Major Arcana cards that everything is as it should be. It may well be another matter if we can see or grasp this, in our time of mourning. It is a reminder that life is still there, it is still happening, regardless of whether our part in it is active or meaningful at this time or not. It shows us that the Universe does not treat us with kid gloves or 'molly coddle' us in any way, it continues to operate to the same laws and ways by which it always has and always will.

We have in this a choice between seeing ourselves as a tiny, insignificant detail that really does not matter and an invitation and option to (continue to) take a role in this grand play in the understanding that what we do has ramifications - our inspirations, thoughts, feelings and actions ripple out and determine the future unfoldment of everything. It may help us to consider that our loved one still does this, although they are not in their physical, earthly, human body any longer.

The energy and experience of this card is life as it is, all of life, and we can rally against it, or 'face and embrace' it. This does not mean we have to like it all, but we do need to learn to accept it as it is. We cannot change outcomes that have already happened but we can change those that have not. We do this by taking that part in our life as the central or leading figure or role. We are the star of our own production called Life and here we are invited to shine.

This can require a great courage and determination as we process and move through our Grief. Each day when we awaken we are reminded of the awful tragedy and loss of our loved one and each day we must accept this. This does not mean we swallow our tears, push down our emotion and 'tough it out'. Rather we tell ourselves that this is ok, we greet our loved one or send them a prayer, perhaps shed a few tears and begin our day. In doing so we can take them with us, honour their memory and the presence we shared in our lives. Each day we accept anew and so embrace the fullness and richness of life and its tragedy, wonder, miracles, inspiration, and above all, Love.

Since my teens I have never seen a purpose in life other than our spiritual growth and development. Everything for me stems from this, and it comes out, I hope, in my experience and relationships. It informs everything in my self and life. Over the forty or so years since I was a teenager, I have come to see that our task in life and the world is to 'walk between the worlds', to aspire to the highest spiritual awareness and growth possible for us, but also to have out feet firmly on this sacred ground and Earth. I like to term this being 'in the world but not of it'. This is the energy available to us with this card and it includes all the scope of life and death. In the end, it is all beautiful.

CHAPTER 5 - MY GRIEF PROCESS

What follows is my personal 'Tarot Mentoring' diary following Laura's death. This follows the practice outlined in Chapter 3. It begins on February 9th, twelve days after the event and continues until August 8th, so covers a six month period. It is included exactly as written, each time I chose a card.

I have a small clear perspex stand on my desk that I slide each card into as I choose it and it stays there until I feel it is time to move on to the next card. This is an entirely intuitive process. Sometimes it is because I want or need something, whether I know what this is or not. Other times it is because it feels like the energy of that card is 'done' in some way. I simply followed the inner prompts as they came.

I have given the date the card was chosen, the card title, the deck I used and the Grief stage it relates to. My responses are presented exactly as written, to give you a true picture of how it worked for me. In all cases what I have written was done as an immediate act, before I looked anything up on the card. Where I have done this it has been mentioned.

I have found the process to be amazingly helpful and therapeutic, and this is why I have included it here; in the hope that it will encourage you to follow your own process in this way, whenever you need to. Reading it back now, it highlights what an amazing thing the Tarot is, with so many synchronicities throughout.

In the Introduction to this book I shared the reason for my writing it. The inclusion of this process attests to that reason, and it felt important to include it, not only for myself but I hope for all those as they navigate their own Grief process. I hope it does due honour to Laura too.

09.0+2 - QUEEN OF WANDS - THELEMA TAROT (ANGER)

I felt almost a resentment at this card when it appeared. I wanted something that showed me my upset, misery, sadness and pain, not someone who is full of strength, life and beans. I wondered if her appearing for me is about the Queen's feistiness, the anger she can have as she is of Fire, but I am not feeling anger (yet), only sadness and loss and an amount of self-pity. The Wands Queen is not this, if anything she is the opposite.

So perhaps she has appeared to tell me that there is life, there can still be passion for living and that irrespective of whatever else happens, we humans are a tough breed, able to withstand the heat of the Fire when it comes like this, rise above the abject pain and misery that our existence can be sometimes and that we experience, and reignite the fire within us that makes us keep going. I certainly need that now.

I cannot help but also liken the card to Laura. Queen of Wands for me is a strong woman, passionate, fierce when necessary, loyal to her cause, whatever it is – nursing and her two boys mainly in Laura's case. She is a woman of strong beliefs who will protect what is hers and what she believes in – Laura certainly had these traits.

I think of all of the Queens as having a big heart as they relate to others through feelings and above all, empathy. Laura had empathy in such huge doses. It was one of her biggest traits and yet could have been a factor in some of her own difficulties, as it can be a big energy to deal with, taking on the energy of other's feelings. This is not something I have considered before with Laura. It certainly made her a large part of who she was, motivated so strongly by her heart, her care and compassion for others. This was demonstrated by her amazing nursing career and also simply in her everyday life, the way she seemed to have the welfare of others in her awareness so much.

More personally for me, that was a big part of our connection, for we share some of that empathy. We certainly knew each other so very well and were so alike is so many ways. Once we had received Amy's cancer diagnosis we became confidants, agreeing to share those black, hard thoughts and fears, no matter what they were. This we did and I like to think we helped each other in this process. She certainly helped me and now I feel, not betrayed, but the loss in that whatever is to come with Amy's illness and how it feels at that vital, inner core level I now have to face alone. There will be plenty of people around me and who will be available, but Laura was the only one that 'got me' (other than Amy of course!).

It strikes me how selfish a process Grief is – of course Laura is the one who's died and it is about her, but my beliefs tell me she is ok now, and continuing her souls' existence. It is those of us still here, that need to deal with the loss and pain of missing her and as I look at this card it does bring a sense of comfort, when I think of her strength within, her determination, gutsy resilience yet still the heart of softness and love within. Laura's hair was dyed a shade of red when she died, maybe that was her inner Queen of Wands on show.

14.02 – PAGE OF PENTACLES – EVERYDAY WITCH TAROT – BARGAINING

This card has the Page standing at a fork in the path he is on and is tossing a coin in the air, as if to decide which way to go. We can see in the background one way leads to the town, the other to a single tower. He stands next to a signpost. I notice the sky above him is blue with white, fluffy clouds, much as they are where I am today. There is a map laid out on the floor in front of him.

I notice the landscape is green around him; grass, trees and fields. The Page Is wearing a green robe and hood, and green leggings. For me green is a colour of healing and I read yesterday that 'grief is a process of healing', something which was profound for me. So much so that I have included it as one of the main quotes to introduce the book. I had thought before that Grief was just something we had to go through when someone died, not that it actually had a purpose. There is comfort in this and something in me (wants to) tell me that Laura is showing me these signs.

From the very many we have of her, thanks mainly to her wonderful sister Kate, I finally chose a photo of Laura that I love and placed it in the frame I bought which is on my desk beside me as I write this. This is the Monday before her funeral on Thursday this week and both Amy and my thoughts are of course filled with this. This is a practical act and so this being a Pentacles card feels right. It is time to focus on this and how it will be and I will be.

We have an aunt and uncle of Amy's staying for two days. I have never met them and whilst I am looking forward to meeting them, I have a concern that I will be playing host when I want to immerse myself in the 'doing' of the funeral and all that goes with it. I am such that I need a good deal of time to be truly myself with people, so the fact of my not having met them before means I may well not. I have already thought that a way around this is to quietly take myself away to my study here for a few minutes when I need to.

So perhaps the signposts are inner ones for me right now, to do what it is I need to in the coming days. If they are outer ones it is about the direction life may take after the funeral. This is a milestone indeed, and there is a stone beside the path like a milestone, which has a pentacle carved on it. It is as if this is a time of power and to take note of it.

The road ahead, or back, after the funeral feels like a yawning chasm now, but will feel different when we get there, as we have to face it. Then it will be about deciding which path to take, which is the one that will lead us – me – forward towards the healing that this Grief process is.

Not having looked at what the book for this deck says about the card until now, I see that it can 'represent one of your children' and speaks of being 'about to begin something different', which in probably an unintended way certainly relates to Laura. It reminds me that the funeral is a time to honour Laura and bid her well on her future path and that this rite of passage is necessary for her. Writing this makes me cry.

19.02 – PAGE OF PENTACLES – EVERYDAY WITCH TAROT – BARGAINING

I wanted to draw another card today, I felt that I wanted to shift the energy I was dealing with. So I did what I always do - placed the previous card back in the deck and shuffled for a while. I fanned the cards out on the floor and picked one that stood out. I got the Page of Pentacles again. I felt an immediate 'ok' but wanted things to move on somehow, so I repeated all the above process and got the same card again! So I went with it this time. It felt good to know I am being guided.

So this is two days after Laura's funeral, which was beautiful and honoured her so well, yet utterly devastating and harrowing too. I sat and talked with Amy the evening after – her aunt and uncle were due to stay then but had to leave due to predictions of a storm coming in the following day with recommendations that travel should not be attempted.

We have talked much since then and today drove out for coffee and cake and talked more. Our conversation focused on those around us and how they are each responding and that if we are to continue our close relationship with Laura's two boys, our grandchildren, we have to make it happen. Amy and I have discussed this and about how we need to establish it and what we can and will do. It feels like a glimpse of something ahead, rather than just getting through each day feeling sad and drained and the focus being only on the death of Laura and everything that flows from that terrible event.

The Page seems to have a say here. It also feels like his energy is getting through in other ways. Amy was talking about 'stepping up' more with her life, making plans to develop friendships and for us to go places we want to visit - Brighton (my home town), London (hers) - as we have said before but since Covid and her cancer diagnosis we have not been able to do. It is like the Page beginning his, or in this case, our, journey.

I am not sure if this is quite Bargaining, but it is certainly a payoff, or a result of a practical response to what we are seeing and sensing within us. I have always thought of the Page of Pentacles as taking the first steps on a journey, a new venture and life certainly feels like that now.

When I mentioned this card to Amy she immediately related it to Laura beginning her new journey - I so often miss the obvious. Everything has changed so much so suddenly and it all looks and feels so different.

23.02 - TEN OF PENTACLES - EVERYDAY WITCH TAROT - BARGAINING

I wanted the energy to keep moving forward, or shift somehow, borne out of a desperation really, or a need to keep going, as I have been forcing myself to do anything these last days, making myself have the motivation. I used the same deck in case the Page wanted to come back again - he didn't - not quite anyway!

There seems a heavy irony to this card, as it features a family and the shift from generations. Immediately before I picked this card I checked our wills as we will now need to update them. This card could be about that – I got the obvious this time!

Earlier today Amy and I discussed how we both felt like our previous fire for life is just not there now, and yet we will not be defeated and give it up. We mentioned that it is exactly one month since Laura was taken to hospital following her lung collapse and cardiac arrest, and was in ICU for four days before she was pronounced dead. The card could again be that, but that also there is life continuing after that awful tragedy and loss.

So the Bargaining here could easily be that, as one life ends so others continue and we must see that, both for ourselves and her two boys, which this card brings clearly to mind. Amy and I have been out twice these last days. It was hard to do but we did it and were glad we did.

More Bargaining here is that it helps to think that Laura was a person who loved her life and doing what she did, and knowing that, she would certainly want us to continue that way.

All of these aspects help, so despite the irony this is a card of things moving forward which I wanted.

25.02 - THE EMPRESS - LIGHT SEERS TAROT - ACCEPTANCE

I shuffled this lovely deck and asked for a card to show me how Amy can be helped, whether by me or herself or anyone. These last few days I have felt an increasing desperation to be of use to her in her abject grief, yet feeling powerless to do so, other than hold her when she cries each day and try to comfort her. She tells me I am her voice of reason which I am pleased at but want to be able to provide some practical help.

The card I received in answer to my question was The Empress – the card of motherhood – precisely the issue, but also exactly what Amy has to grieve, the loss of this to Laura. There seems an irony again here, or of pathos and it could be easy to think that the Tarot is playing games with me. But I know the Tarot better than that.

Thinking to my own army of strategies and exercises, it comes to me that Amy could write about being Laura's Mum. She could write whatever comes to her but my impulse was to write it as a celebration of what was good about it, but it could certainly include whatever Amy needs it to. My sense is of Amy focusing on the celebration of Laura, just as some kind of small antidote to the dark abyss it seems she is in, quite understandably. I do not wish to rescue her, no-one can do that really, but to offer a rope to grasp if she wishes, to begin to pull herself out of that deep well that surrounds and towers above her.

There could be many other aspects to this card but this is a place to start. I will see if I can find an appropriate space to share it with Amy and 'put it out there'. I feel like it is a vain hope really, but at least it's something, if not for her, for me.

28.02 - PRINCESS (PAGE) OF SWORDS - HEAVEN AND EARTH TAROT - DENIAL

A Swords card is not a surprise as I think I am still firmly in denial. Not because I am pretending Laura is still alive or anything like that, but because it just does not seem real and in my head I keep expecting to see her sometime, or get a text from her. This is despite consciously knowing she is dead - I was there when she was pronounced dead and was at the funeral. Yet still this sense persists. There is a weird comfort, until you remember it's not real.

Looking at this card, the Princess is holding her sword aloft in a windy place, as if to stand her ground and declare she can withstand the winds, and rain too going by the dark clouds above her. She is quite alone, which feels fitting as I am very aware of my aloneness at the moment. There are people around but none close that I can fully be open with in my situation – Laura was that.

That the Princess is 'standing her ground' seems right. I have been mindful of making myself do the things I would usually do. There is little motivation to do so, but I sense I need to keep putting one foot in front of another and there is then a hope that the current sense of apathy and lack of motivation will pass and some sense of passion for life, might return some day.

02.03 - ACE OF RAINBOWS (PENTACLES) - OSHO ZEN TAROT - BARGAINING

The last couple of days I have been aware of a huge emptiness within myself, and externally of Laura's absence. When shuffling this deck I asked for a card to show me how to respond to this and help me with it.

This is the Ace of Pentacles. As such I can see how the energy I need to employ is simply putting one foot in front of the other, keeping going, doing things, however small. There is a suggestion in my mind as I consider the card that there is a future path ahead, even though I cannot see it and right now have no idea what it might be, or feel a sense of positive hope for 'happiness' in it.

I find the actual image for this card hard to relate to, but this deck does take a somewhat different approach to mine. It speaks of an awakened being, in the moment and of the 'eternal spring' within our being. It is good to know it is there at least, even if I am not aware of it right now.

I take from this card a message and energy that says 'just keep going, you can do this' and that alone is a help.

06.03 - TEN OF SWORDS - TAROT DE LA NUIT - DENIAL

I took a card today out of a sense of being very low, with thoughts of my grieving of what has been lost – apart from

Laura, but of the lifestyle Amy and I had and loved before her cancer diagnosis. I recall evenings when we would sit and one of us might say 'I do love our lives'. So much has gone since then and it is now about getting through the day – existing rather than living, something I have always fought against. I asked for a card for what I need for this.

As I took the deck out of its box I saw that the bottom card was the Ten of Swords and thought 'yep, that's me'. I shuffled the deck in my usual style and asked for what I was drawing a card for. I fanned them out face down, took the one that stood out for me and it was the Ten of Swords.

The image of this card reminds me a little of John Everett Millais' painting of Ophelia from Shakespeare's Hamlet. Ophelia lays in the river having been driven mad by Hamlet's murder of her father and is 'incapable of her own distress'. This card is as if it shows just the head and shoulders from the picture, as a lady lies in dark water, her face above the water line, her long hair billowing out beneath. There is a glowing blue/green light between an arch of two trees.

The image gives me a sense both of the gloom and loss I feel, the inner, inexpressible nature of my thoughts and sensation and of calm isolation surrounding all that. As I consider it further I see the gaze is directed upwards and sends me a sense of hope. Her thoughts – in the back of her head - are submerged in dark water – my deep, sad, grieving emotions, yet I can still look up, see a glowing light, a subtle, none too clear as yet, light of hope. I am reminded of Oscar Wilde's quote 'We are all in the gutter, some of us are looking at the stars'.

11.03 - PAGE OF WANDS - TAROT DE LA NUIT - ANGER

The days prior to today were ones of just feeling sad and fighting apathy, other than wanting to write the Tarot for

Grief book as part of my therapy and to gain a sense of use in my life. However, other demands meant I could not, and still cannot do any of it.

Today however I woke and when I tuned into myself felt something approaching anger. I say this because anger is not something that comes naturally to me – other than with myself when my tennis strokes are off! Yet today I could feel a sense of frustration or anger. Not at anything or anyone specific, but of the feeling just being there without a focus. I could visualize myself standing on the beach and yelling, that kind of anger.

So I took a card for this and received the Page of Wands. I was not at all surprised it was a Wand, and in some ways felt relief that I was correctly sensing myself at least. The Page immediately suggested this was the beginning of a process to work through, which does not fill me with pleasure.

In this deck the Page is that of a young blond woman who has a fire and a passion in her eyes. Her face and hair seem to be floating amidst an eerie glow, set in trees at night. The booklet with this deck subtitles this card as 'A Night to Begin Again' which feels apt, if we only could after someone's death.

It speaks of not fearing the night, which beautifully reminds me of the song 'Look at the Night' which my friend Luke wrote about me some years ago, and which he reminded me of some lyrics from last week. I played it then and will do so again. It helps and anything that does is worth doing.

The Page of Wands is about following her passion and acting on it. Mine at present is the Tarot for Grief book, but perhaps I need to widen that at least to my other work that I still have going on and be grateful that I do still have that – turn anger to passion and then action. It feels like a challenge.

14.03 – SIX OF WANDS – LAW OF ATTRACTION TAROT – ANGER

I have been fighting apathy, out of a sense of the drudgery of each day and also of 'preparatory grief' with Amy – we face scan results to see what may be happening with her cancer tomorrow. It feels like everything is in abeyance and that life has sunk into a morass of just doing.

So not a surprise to receive a Wand again. The image from this innovative deck has a farmer reaping a field of wheat – reaping what has been sown of course, but I fail to see how I am doing that really. Perhaps it is about my current actions and how they are creating a future of prolonged apathy and drudgery if I do not shift it. I do make myself do things most of the time, or the things that have to be done, but need to place more focus on such things as my daily morning yoga – too tempting to lay there with a cup of tea and watch the repeated clips of horrors from Ukraine as the Russian army continue their invasion now.

The book here speaks of the 'risk of living' which feels apt, that I need to take this, and that it is already there in a different sense. I am reminded of the quote from The Shawshank Redemption film to 'get busy living or get busy dying'. This is how I see the figure in this card which I shall determine to be and do.

18.03 – THREE OF WANDS – LAW OF ATTRACTION TAROT – ANGER

The card above has been useful as a reminder to me to get things done and keep going each day, which I have been doing, given the guidance from this card. Now I want whatever's next, not from a 'that's done, next please' place but in order to avoid any stagnation and because I need it.

This time I move from the 6 to the 3 of Wands and here the image is of a farmer sowing seed, rather than harvesting. I take from this that I need to focus on what I am sowing, and need to, before I can read the rewards. This suggests to me my inner attitude, rather than practical actions, although they apply as a result. Interestingly, I plan to do some gardening to tidy our garden up tomorrow, and plant some grass seed!

I have been firing on some good cylinders these last days with creative Tarot ideas, though not much time for developing them or acting on them, but it has been good to connect with that sense and feeling, so this cards energy ties in there and it is good to know I am being fed this way. It is a great follow on from the place of just doing each day, which I have been trying to fight. It helps that the Sun is shining today, it is blue skies and the brightness is refreshing.

23.03 - THREE OF SWORDS - TAROT ILLUMINATI - DENIAL

The last few days have been good ones – the Sun has been shining, there is some warmth in it and it feels like Spring is here and I have been outside more. I therefore approached the deck and asked for what I need now for myself and received this card.

I am not surprised to have received a Sword – despite the days being good I have been aware of thoughts in my mind at various times of Laura and sadness relating to her, as well as 'preparatory grief' thoughts on Amy – she is scheduled for surgery soon to remove a tumour plus the adrenal gland it is on. We are told it is 'not a big deal' but the implications are still there.

An initial response to this card is that I have been fooling myself, telling myself I am doing good when really the sadness is still there. Of course it is, but so is the attitude from above, of getting things going and doing things, which I have been. Swords 3 is one of those cards that people make assumptions on because of the image – swords stuck into a heart.

That it is Swords and so mental makes sense as the 'battle' I have been aware of these last days has indeed been in my head. I seem to keep checking mentally if Laura's death feels real yet, mainly because I think it is slowly sinking in and a part of me does not want it to.

It would be easy to go with this but for me the energy of the number 3 is a creative, productive one. I have found it can indicate when there is conflict between the head and heart, and this sums my sense up perfectly. My sense is that this card is showing me the need to blend both – each have their place and need but my sense of self and power comes from a blending of head and heart that results in inner strength, focus, determination etc. There is the thought here that this is about being kind to myself and my needs, in head and heart.

28.03 – SEVEN OF CUPS – TAROT OF THE HIDDEN REALM – DEPRESSION

Yesterday was Mother's Day in the UK, the first time we have dealt with this since Laura's death, and it will be the first of many such occasions and anniversaries. We had planned to see our grandchildren and their Dad, along with our daughter Kate and son in law Bogdan. One of the young boys had a cough though and in Amy's perilous immune condition we can take no chances, so it was just Kate and Bogdan. We had a lovely time and delivered a picnic for the other three to their door instead.

We did acknowledge how we felt and we feel we coped with the day well and yet in the evening there was a palpable quiet and deep sadness, perhaps from the emotional drain of the day. For me this persisted this morning and was the under-current for all I have been doing. So I asked for a card to respond to this. No surprise to see a Cup appearing in this case.

In this deck there is an elfin male who looks as if he is sitting contemplating and looks quite sad. There are seven stars around him, which I like, in the leaves and branches he is sat amongst. My initial response is that this looks how I feel. What comes to me is a reminder that I can, or need, to choose how I feel, and not let my feelings control me. Just having this message in my mind is a help. It does not deny my feeling, nor can I or want to do this, but it does tell me I can acknowledge it but not let it have dominion over me.

It also reminds me that there are other feelings, and that all of them come and go. Each in their own way contributes to me and my being and how this is and will continue to evolve as all things must do, and I move onwards and forwards with myself and my life.

01.04 – THE WHEEL – TAROT DE LA NUIT – ACCEPTANCE

I have been acutely aware of the loss of Laura these last couple of days, and yet still is does not seem real. So I asked for a card to help me with it becoming real, since I know it needs to at some point. It was not a surprise then to receive a Major card for this, being Acceptance, since this is what I am seeking to do, as a way of moving forwards a bit.

There are three different women on this card, each linked by a red thread – the web of life as I see it – the life-force – each looking in different directions. This brings to mind the Three Fates and this feels very fitting here. This tells me there are bigger and stronger, greater forces than just me at work here, and as the booklet says, they know what they are doing.

The sense and message I get here is one of 'going with the flow'. I cannot force myself to make it real, though I want this to happen so I can come to terms with it more. I expect in doing this I am looking for a way out of the pain of it. The Wheel however, will surely turn and will do so in its own time.

06.04 – STRENGTH – EVERYDAY ENCHANTMENT TAROT – ACCEPTANCE

I have been acutely aware of the hole in myself and my life, both from Laura's death and the enforced change of lifestyle Amy and I have had to shift to following her cancer diagnosis as well as the impact of Covid. I therefore asked for a card to help me with what I do about this hole, how do I adjust to it?

As I phrased this question in my mind I did wonder as I shuffled the deck whether this was pointing towards an acceptance, of the 'hole', in some way. It was not surprising then, to receive a Major card.

I was reading about this card yesterday, about how it can be to do with a need for compassion for ourselves to accept ourselves as we are, embracing our faults, failures and 'fuck-ups' rather than trying to hide from them or pretend they are not there. This is where our Strength can lie. It reminded me of making a friend of our enemies.

The card in this deck has a lady in a wheelchair with her arms aloft, a large dog beside her (rather than the lion), which perhaps symbolises loyalty and friendship, to and for the self. There is what looks like a spiral of fire energy that is rippling out all around her, for me indicating the effect this attitude and approach can have.

Synchronistically, as I was going through my process with this card a song played called 'It Is What It Is', which seems entirely appropriate for this. This is in a spirit of acceptance rather than resentment or resignation, or even acquiescence. Rather it is an active thing, something that I can use, not to plug and just fill the hole, but at this stage, look into and see what is there that I can learn from and grow.

11.04 - EIGHT OF CUPS - WITCHES TAROT - DEPRESSION

Laura was on the organ donor's register. We know that her liver, kidneys and heart were donated. Yesterday we received a letter from the recipient of her heart. This was both beautiful and (more than) bittersweet. For me it brought the sadness of it all back. Although, as the letter stated its new 'owner' is now caring for Laura's heart and it is caring for her, which is truly lovely, I cannot help but feel sadness at such a special heart as Laura had, in the emotional rather than physical sense, being used by someone else, as lovely as this person sounds. I asked for a card for this.

Cups Eight is a card that can often be about leaving behind an emotional experience and 'moving on'. This is not as easy as that of course – when is it ever? My sense is that we can only ever move on when we are able to 'face and embrace' the full force and weight of what we are feeling, and only then be able to release it. For me this card is telling me it is Ok to feel sad about this – I feel a bit guilty at my sadness, since it is based on someone's life being saved. So I will cry about this and the loss of my darling girl, with the reminder too, as the figure in the card looks at a crescent Moon, that amidst the departure and loss, there is still beauty and love. This is part of Laura's legacy and that's a damn good one.

18.04 - FOUR OF CUPS - LIGHT SEERS TAROT - DEPRESSION

This card was taken just prior to Laura's husband and boys and our other daughter Kate and fiancé Bogdan visiting us for Easter. I sense a tension in myself at this time, being a chance for family gathering and Laura's absence so noticeable, as well as an ongoing sadness I cannot shake, from being aware of the absence of Laura from our lives as well as Amy's health which is not good now, as we await an operation for her, plus the limits on our lives as a result, with Covid still prevalent too.

So no surprise to receive another Cup and this one certainly expresses my inner feeling of late. On this image I am struck by the (mostly) red tide of energy as I perceive it rising from one of the Cups, as if the figure in the card is losing her will. There is however a good, strong Oak tree in the background on the horizon and I am drawn to this as a symbol of strength and power. I need to find and force the will power within me to rise, tap into the help from the tree kingdom – almost 'fake it till I make it'. It feels like an ongoing battle at present.

26.04 - KNIGHT OF CUPS - LIGHT SEERS TAROT - DEPRESSION

The feelings I was having that gave me the Four of Cups above have remained, albeit underneath my everyday self, which is really quite cheery! I asked a basic 'what do I need now' in selecting this card. Again the same suit follows on.

I love this deck for many reasons, one being its modern look. Here the Knight is a cool dude sitting on a stool holding a bunch of roses, looking as if he is waiting for his love to arrive, with a blanket with fruit and wine waiting. His horse paws the ground impatiently in the background.

What I get immediately from this card is not to sit around waiting, but to go for it and get on with living. I am trying to do this as much as is possible given the practical situation with Amy, as we await surgery for her cancer and she is not feeling good. I have been feeling cut off from the outside world, and connection with the natural world. I cannot leave her for long periods of time on her own, so getting out on my bike, running or playing tennis have become my salvation for these things.

The other thought I had here was that of the need for loving myself. Again, I am doing what I can with this when possible, in terms of doing the things I love and what I need to keep as healthy as possible. I have always said love is the strongest energy there is, and this Knight lives with this all the time. His is an energy I can tap into, which I shall do as the card remains on my desk now.

03.05 - TWO OF CUPS - EVERYDAY WITCH TAROT - DEPRESSION

Today is Laura's birthday and my overriding feeling is really just sadness, and a longing to be with her to mark the day. Amy and I had a conversation the other day and agreed that it seems the more time is going on the more we miss her. I reasoned that this may lessen as more time goes on, but it certainly makes sense right now.

I picked a card because it is Laura's day and in terms of the above sense. This has two people sat on chairs on a beautiful beach with a setting sun toasting each other with a drink and gazing at each other. It is a lovely scene and seems perfectly logical for the occasion, so I shall do this for Laura later. I notice how the shadows from the people lie on the foreground, which seems poetically apt too.

I take from this to celebrate the good things from Laura and the connection we shared so well. Happy Birthday my darling girl.

07.05 - FIVE OF CUPS - TAROT DE LA NIUT - DEPRESSION

This is the fifth card in a row over the last month that Cups has appeared for me. This certainly seems apt since I have been feeling a deep sadness inside. This is not preventing me from living my life or fulfilling the daily activities I want to do, and neither am I on the verge of tears all the time, or not laughing and so on. However, within me there is always a sense of a deep and profound sadness and loss.

This card was taken a couple of days after getting the news that Amy now has a cancerous brain tumor and faces further chemotherapy treatment and all that goes with it. The card features a mermaid sitting on top of a rock above a pool, looking at a ship in the distance, with dark clouds all around.

The sense of this image is one of (perhaps self-imposed) isolation and longing. Ultimately, this card can be about choosing how we respond to that feeling – letting the sadness and loss overwhelm and consume us, or choose to accept it, allow it to be what it is and keep choosing hope. I cannot sense this at present where Amy's health is concerned, only that whatever happens there is not a time of prolonged suffering for her and that the future is not traumatic for us both, however that may play out.

In the meantime it is good to know and be reminded I can choose and will use the message of this card as best I can.

16.05.22 - QUEEN OF SWORDS - LAW OF ATTRACTION TAROT - DENIAL

A couple of days after the last card was chosen I was directed to a meditation a Tarot student had created on Grief, and this created a profound sadness within me, which felt deep and at my core. This stayed the rest of that day and after a night of strong dreams I felt distinctly lighter in myself, which has remained. I asked for what I needed now for this card.

This somewhat different deck has two girls in a tug of war, which looks more a game than a war. They are on a beach with the Sun shining. In this deck the card is subtitled 'The Rival'. For me this has a message of a tug of war in my own mind, arguing with myself mentally. I have been thinking of late, and reading in a book on Grief about finding meaning in it, how my response to the death I have experienced has really been to focus on my life and its meaning and purpose, galvanizing me into action. Yet, with Amy about to begin more chemotherapy, there will be little time and energy to do the things for myself I cherish. Of course caring for her and time with her is absolutely cherished, especially now but for my personal goals, which is my work with Tarot mainly, I am mentally conflicted.

All I can really do, it seems to me, is take the chances that arise, ensuring I keep my priorities clear, that being Amy of course, and maintaining my own well-being and the things I do for that. I hope for anyone reading this that does not sound selfish or callous. I have people around me who tell me I must keep myself going and doing the things I need and can for my own well-being, in order to best support Amy, and this is what I am trying to do.

22.05.22 - THE EMPEROR - EVERYDAY ENCHANTMENT TAROT - ACCEPTANCE

This card was taken on the first available time I had following the start of Amy's second round of chemotherapy. Yesterday evening we shared our feelings of deep sadness that lie beneath our everyday selves now, with both her treatment and the loss of Laura. I said that I felt as if I was mirroring her at times, in the way that people can when they spend so much time together, which we are, like women who live together find their periods happening at the same time. Sometimes I think I am experiencing the physical pains she gets, like a husband going through his wife's birthing pains or some such.

The card has a modern business man in a suit at a desk, one arm outstretched and smiling, as if he is greeting us and wants to shake our hand. It is night time as the window behind him shows a full moon and a bird flying. There is a family photo on the wall.

There is a sense of acceptance in this stage Amy and I are at and I have been thinking the last few days of how I have come to be more accepting of our present life-style, so different to how we used to be. This was confirmed in Amy's chemo treatments starting again and the return of all that goes with it. Different, but not better. Someone who drove us to the hospital - Amy is not allowed to drive with a tumour in the brain and I do not – asked me as she drove me home again how I was getting on with it all now – I said that we've got used to it, no idea how long Amy will be here but that is has become our norm now.

In acknowledging this I find in this card a sense of the ownership and governance of The Emperor of how our life is. This does not mean I like it and certainly not welcoming of it as he is in the card, but still with owning what our lives are, which feels a positive thing, at least to some degree.

27.05.22 - SEVEN OF WANDS - EVERYDAY ENCHANTMENT TAROT - ANGER

In this deck this card shows a group of women defending a wood and protesting about its presumed planned destruction. The seven and familiar yellow-coated police/security men are lined up before them. This immediately brings back memories of the Twyford Down road protests I took part in, in the 90's.

This brings to mind the concept of 'righteous anger' and suggest it is ok to be angry about Laura's death. I do not really connect with that feeling, but I can, to some degree about Amy's condition and her having to go through chemotherapy again, which is happening as I write this. In all honesty, it is not so much that she has cancer, but the impact on her, seeing her suffering as she is and the basic removal of our lifestyle. Sure I think we have done a pretty good job of adapting to it, but there is a deep regret, more than anger really, I have been sensing lately that I need to do the things that fit in with our adapted lifestyle now, that I can for myself, for my own well-being, which I am doing.

One thought that has just occurred is that I am angry about the loss of my/our Tarot business – we spent 8 years building up a recognised and successful practice together, to build on what I already had and I will have to start again at some point. So be it. I think perhaps that is what my continued writing about the life-style change and so on has at its root.

The card can also points towards the 'battle' Amy is in, against her cancer. I said to her many months ago now, that I don't like the idea of a 'battle' (in obituaries it's always, "after a brave fight and battling cancer") and the term suggest it's a win or lose situation, where there will ultimately only ever be one winner, in Amy's case at least. Yes, it is a battle, but this has helped me to recognise that what my saying this is about is my seeing her going through prolonged suffering and becoming slowly more debilitated. For me, that ain't no battle. For me, it is about learning to adapt and live with it, in the best way possible. Like so many things, so easy to say, so hard to do.

02.06.22 - KING OF SWORDS - EVERDAY ENCHANTMENT TAROT - DENIAL

These last two days I have been experiencing what came to my mind before I took a card for a response to it - 'stabbing pains' of grief – sudden, unexpected, and uncalled for piercing shards of sadness and emptiness, and just plain missing Laura. It is in those times that I think, or even 'know' there will never be anything that can put this right or make it go away, which seems to compound the sadness. I know it is a case of learning to accept it, but right now, that seems like the worst part of it.

So it seems, yet again, entirely fitting that I get a Swords card, given the stabbing analogy that came to me. In this brilliant deck we have an image of a lawyer, presenting his case in court to a rapt colleague and jury who listen intently. The Sword in question seems to be an exhibit, perhaps the murder weapon.

I find it interesting that there is half a glass of water on the table before him. This seems to bring the question of whether it is half full or half empty – cliché this may be, but an apt one for my position now. Swords King for me is all about the mind, mental control and agility, but there is often a link between the head and heart – what is in our mind is often because of what is in our heart. This seems to be the case for me, as in my first paragraph for this card. My sense is that this card is reminding me of this heart/head interplay and my need to be conscious of this and how it is working within me.

This will not, cannot, take away the pain of course, but it can help me manage it.

NB I have stayed with the same deck having seen the very sad news of Poppy Palin, the deck's creator, having taken her own life a few days ago. Journey well Poppy.

08.06.22 – SEVEN OF SWORDS – SPELLCASTERS TAROT – DENIAL

Here we have a man who seems to be creeping away in the night from a fire, with six of the seven swords in his arms. There are two wolves/dogs sleeping by the fire, with the other sword lying on the ground. The mood is of stealth, stealing and secrets.

Given that the Swords are about my thinking, this would seem to suggest that I need to take what I have learned/am learning from all this. I have been so mindful this last week of the things Laura did not get to do and how those of us around her are impacted by this too, as well as how my and Amy's lives have had to change so much and what we cannot do in the face of her condition now.

It seems relevant that the sword left behind here is right beside the fire. If the man picks this up it will likely burn his hand, so there is a suggestion not to dwell on or bring with me that which is harmful in my mind. I do keep reminding myself of these things in the hope they will become habit. Most of the time this works but there are of course times when they do not, which I allow.

I gain a sense of comfort from this card - the glow and the light from the fire is lovely.

20.06 – I have been sitting with this card as it has connected me to something of a repeating pattern in my thoughts, which I do not feel I can share with anyone. The outlet for them would only have been Laura. Yesterday was Fathers' Day and I felt her close, which was lovely, but acutely painful too. I remain guardian over my thoughts, like the wolves in the card.

29.06 - KNIGHT OF SWORDS - ARCANUM TAROT - DENIAL

I sat with the previous card for some time while I observed the thought patterns I have been having and sought to come to terms with them. Now it feels time for the next card. The thought I put to the deck was simply 'what's next'?

I responded with a wry nod at having another Swords card. That it is the Knight gives me a good feeling though. I see he is in full armour, the visor on his helmet down and he seems to be steaming ahead on his horse. My thoughts have been very much about focusing on living life, with purpose and intent, the 'carpe diem' approach, now clichéd but no less true and powerful. This chap seems to embody that for me right now and it is good to have him with me.

11.07 – I have been mindful of this card throughout his time on my desk with me. There have been some small but painful occurrences that have highlighted Laura's absence, and the Knight feels like he is there as an advocate for me, urging me onwards despite the pain and sorrow and facing the unknown ahead where Amy is concerned.

17.07. - SEVEN OF SWORDS - TAROT DE LA NUIT - DENIAL

I was surprised to receive another Sword, and the same card as I had before the Knight I just had. My first thought was to consider if I am denying anything, Swords being the Grief stage of Denial. My first response to this is that I am consciously focusing on Amy and maintaining positivity – for her primarily and then myself. I have wondered in my head lately where after Amy's death, whenever that will be, whether a much bigger/deeper wave of Grief will emerge from within me that has not been able to, or I have not allowed after Laura's death, due to Amy's condition and my necessary focus on that. I short I wonder if I am carrying around a deeper level of Grief all the time, weighing me down.

This card image is quite different to the previous Swords 7. It shows a woman fleeing a house under the moonlight. There seems to be a woman behind her who may be asking her what is wrong and why she is going. These strike me of the two parts of my mind I have been experiencing lately – one where the majority of the time I am ok with life and what has happened and will happen. Then the other where I think I am so sad within and have only more to come and what I will have to face. I know I will face this and my mind keeps expecting the worst to happen by way of trying to prepare myself for it. The reality is that I can't fully prepare and can only experience what happens when it does.

Either way it is much for the mind to deal with and the mental energy can be a drain, with inner thoughts I do not really have a healthy outlet for as things stand now. I am finding the inner peace of meditation invaluable now.

29.07 - SEVEN OF SWORDS - KNIGHT TEMPLAR TAROT

The same card, once more! This is from a new deck I bought myself and I did my usual thing with a brand new deck, of 'washing' the deck first (swirling all the card about on the floor with both hands to give them a real mix). I then gathered them up and shuffled and did my usual focusing and asked for the card I need next. This was the result!

My first response to this is to be disappointed and a bit angry! I wanted to move on, but this tells me I am not ready/able. The very fact that this is my first response confirms this.

This image is different again. It shows a 'corrupt Muslim' letting Templars into a door into the Tower of Antioch. The last card I wrote for the 'Tarot for Grief' book was The Tower so this seems oddly fitting. Perhaps there are some good Templars I need to let into me/my Tower, symbols of the best mindset I can have.

The commentary for this card suggest that a 'negative element can turn out to be useful'. It suggests to me that I need to keep working on my mind and how I perceive things. It reminds me that I keep expecting the worst, which as I said above I realise is to try and prepare for what is ahead. I am reading a book now on 'Mindful Tarot' which tells us to be only in the present moment and that 'Nothing is hidden, Nothing is broken'. These seem very applicable for me now, as does the continued importance of my meditation practice which is the best thing I know to maintain the inner place and equilibrium I need.

It is now six months since Laura's death. It feels like yesterday and whilst the sadness and pain may not be at the surface of my heart and mind quite as much, the acuteness of it and the sense of missing her is. It feels like this is just how it is now – most of the time I am fine, but now and again there is this reality that surfaces.

Amy and I spoke yesterday of how we have really been in 'limbo land' since her diagnosis, a state of not knowing what is happening -

- in her body with the cancer
- what the treatment she has had is doing and if it is working
- what the pain she gets may be indicating
- what the results of the latest scans will be
- how long she will be able to have/tolerate treatment
- what will happen when she does not have treatment for whatever reason
- how long she has left to live

Those are what come to mind as I write this and there could be more. This seems to fit the need of being in that present moment. My sense is a need for acceptance in my mind of everything how it is, the loss of Laura, the pain and sadness of this now, Amy's 'health', our lives and how we (have to) live them now.

08.08 - THE EMPRESS - LIGHT SEERS TAROT

I have been sensing a shift in my mindset from the above and so it felt like the right time to draw the next card. I have to admit to an immediate sense of being pleased both that it was not a Sword and that it is a Major card.

My first response here is that of it being in keeping with my sense of 'what comes next'. This is with regard to both the mourning of Laura's death and Amy's situation. We have a three week wait for scan results as we speak which will determine what is happening with her tumours and whether further treatment is needed and/or possible.

I notice first on this lovely image that The Empress is shown apparently heavily pregnant, with the Earth in her belly. This suggests to me that anything is possible and that it will happen in its own time, when it is ready to.

I looked up what I wrote in the book on this card - I never remember what I have written - I have no idea if other authors have this - and I speak about care, for the self and others, as well as the energy of Love. In all this I am sensing a shift, away from the prime focus on the grief over Laura and to Amy and to our situation here. I am mindful of the caring role I have and all that comes with it, plus the inevitable outcome we have been told of. I speak about being in the moment with the energy of this card as the focus of self-care and love, and this seems to be what is required now.

This card seems to bring about the subject of 'preparatory grief' for me, something I need to know more of.

~ ~ ~ ~ ~ ~ ~ ~ ~ ~ ~

At the end of Chapter 3 I suggested creating a table of the cards chosen through your Tarot for Grief mentoring process. Here is mine from the cards above. Just a brief look at this showed me something I was not aware of as I lived it. This is the remarkable way in which the cards show how in general I experience a stage, reach acceptance of it, then move on to the next. In my case it was Bargaining, Anger, Depression and Denial, but there is no correct or preferred order we should or should not have them.

DATE	CARD	STAGE
09.02	QUEEN OF WANDS	ANGER
14.02	PAGE OF PENTACLES	BARGAINING
19.02	PAGE OF PENTACLES	BARGAINING
23.02	TEN OF PENTACLES	BARGAINING
25.02	THE EMPRESS	ACCEPTANCE

28.02	PAGE OF SWORDS	DENIAL
02.03	ACE OF PENTACLES	BARGAINING
06.03	TEN OF SWORDS	DENIAL
11.03	PAGE OF WANDS	ANGER
14.03	SIX OF WANDS	ANGER
18.03	THREE OF WANDS	ANGER
23.03	THREE OF SWORDS	DENIAL
28.03	SEVEN OF CUPS	DEPRESSION
01.04	WHEEL OF FORTUNE	ACCEPTANCE
06.04	STRENGTH	ACCEPTANCE
11.04	EIGHT OF CUPS	DEPRESSION
18.04	FOUR OF CUPS	DEPRESSION
26.04	KNIGHT OF CUPS	DEPRESSION
03.05	TWO OF CUPS	DEPRESSION
07.05	FIVE OF CUPS	DEPRESSION
16.05	QUEEN OF SWORDS	DENIAL
22.05	EMPEROR	ACCEPTANCE
27.05	SEVEN OF WANDS	ANGER
02.06	KING OF SWORDS	DENIAL
08.06	SEVEN OF SWORDS	DENIAL
29.06	KNIGHT OF SWORDS	DENIAL
17.07	SEVEN OF SWORDS	DENIAL
29.07	SEVEN OF SWORDS	DENIAL
08.08	THE EMPRESS	ACCEPTANCE

This also shows that I received more Swords cards than any other, suggesting Denial was the strongest or biggest issue for me. I agree with this, in that it still amazes me that it happened at all, and things still serve as a reminder that it did, rather than it being a simple fact as yet. This one will take some time to fully accept I think.

The lowest number of cards from a suit was Pentacles, and these all occurred together, in the first four cards chosen. This shows that any Bargaining I had to do was done early on, and always seems a fruitless exercise to me ultimately.

I experienced every number and Court card at least once, apart from a Nine, suggesting that Grief needs to flow through the whole gamut of our experience and self. The highest occurrence was a Seven, perhaps making sense with the associations here of fate, destiny and so on. There were four Pages, showing the learning and growth possible through it all.

CHAPTER 6 - TAROT FOR HEALING GRIEF

For me it has become so vital to understand and accept that I will not 'get over' the loss of Laura's death, in the same way that an addict, of whatever kind, is never cured - they are always an addict, it is only whether they are 'using' or not. In the same way the acceptance that Grief cannot be cured or a stage reached where it is all done and dealt with, is an empowering one. In doing so we gain dominion over it, rather than the other way round. It is in this sense that the process of Grief is ultimately one of healing.

Our Grief can become part of us, not as an ever present, unspoken, underlying sadness, but something that we experienced and have come to accept and understand. This does not make it easy each time it should happen and that we just need to follow the process through until we feel we have accepted the loss. Whenever a loved one dies we have to feel the full force of the loss, mourn for them and allow our bereavement its expression.

This is an individual thing and there is no right or wrong way, or length of time it should or should not take. What matters is that we do it, rather than leave it unexpressed, or back away from it through fear at what might happen when we do. It is then that it can become harmful.

Grief is something that seems also to need to effect every level of us as human beings - physical, emotional, mental and spiritual. Tears need to be shed, questions need to be asked, memories shared, objects viewed and held, and so much more. In opening ourselves to the process of Grief it has to take effect at each part and level of our being for us to truly find a sense of healing through it.

For me, it was natural to turn to the Tarot in my Grief as part of my process and mostly in an attempt to understand how to navigate through it all and try to find and give some meaning to it. I do not mean a meaning to Laura's death - I think that only she can fully know that - but a meaning to my Grief, what is happening, what to do with it, to let it happen and come to understand this about me and this part of my life and experience.

Through its constituent parts the Tarot has the ability to relate to each of the aforementioned levels of the human being. It also has the ability to reach the greater holistic truth of our entirety, or soul. It is this that for me makes it the ideal companion on a journey into and through our Grief. My long experience of working with the Tarot has shown me that it will always tell the truth, as the saying goes, it pulls no punches. It will respond honestly to the questions we put to it. It is capable of ultimate understanding, since it is really a reflection of the underlying and formative, energetic truth of our self and being. When we approach it with this in mind we can see how we can entrust all aspects of our self to its knowledge and guidance.

In the preceding chapter I have shared the process the Tarot took me through in my Grief. This is not completed or finished of course - I do not know if it ever will be really, but right now after a six month period and as I reach the end of writing this book, it feels like a good place to stop with regard to what gets included here. If you have read through it all you may have noticed how the subject of Amy's illness and condition seems to have become gradually more an issue as the diary progressed.

We cannot separate our Grief from the rest of our life. It is not something we can compartmentalize and open ourselves to only when we choose or feel like it. It pervades the whole of our being and our life. It is again, only by allowing it to do so that we can reach a place of healing in it. Also again, it is the Tarot that is I think, uniquely placed to do this.

I have also made mention of the subject of Preparatory Grief. My sense is that this is far more common than is perhaps realised. Of course in Laura's case there was no warning or indication of any impending death, but in many cases there is. Sometimes, as with Amy, we can be told that a condition is 'incurable', but it is not possible (and arguably advisable) to put a finite time to this. At most there can be an approximation.

Either way, my experience is that once we are given this knowledge – of an impending death, not a time to it - we begin a process of Grief. This may or may not be conscious, but it can happen nonetheless. So much of how this occurs depends on the individuals involved of course, and the relationships between them. The shift in focus that I noticed when I read back through the previous chapter, essentially from Laura to Amy, made me aware of the Preparatory Grief I have been involved in, party to, and part of. This is happening in many ways and at many levels.

It may well be the case that this is what continues in my process with the Tarot from here onwards. The fact that Preparatory Grief exists at all can show us that Grief is not about the person who has died, is dying or will die, but the one that mourns them. This makes it possible to engage in our Grief before the event and can of course in this way help us prepare for it which in turn can then help us after it as well. This does not necessarily make it easier, but as I hope I have made clear, it is something we must do and need to do, and here is a way and means that we can, and with the aid and input of the Tarot, do so in a more informed, guided and understanding way.

It should also be said that Grief is not only concerned with the death of someone we love in our lives. We can need to grieve from all manner of things, and in effect, anything that has meaning for us. This may be somewhere we live, a job or career, friendship or relationship, hobby or interest and so on. I have mentioned how I have found myself grieving the loss of the lifestyle Amy and I had that changed so suddenly and dramatically, once with the diagnosis of her cancer, and then again on Laura's death.

This is a process that can also take effect on the different levels of our being, and in different ways in our life. Again, what can matter most is that we recognise our need to grieve the loss, or change, and in so doing come to acceptance and full adjustment to it. In this way we can move fully and consciously into the next stage of what we engage in within both our self and life, or inwardly and outwardly. The Tarot can also play the same guiding, explanatory and ultimately healing role for us and with us.

Grief needs to be seen as a process of healing, despite the tragedy and awfulness of the reason for it being there in the first place. If we can open ourselves to this concept, even if at first we do not believe it, then we can allow ourselves, with use of the Tarot, to be accompanied by a friend who truly knows us, who will not lie to us, will give us the truth and then respect our options and choices and will always have our well-being, growth and healing as the first, and really the only, priority.

For me, not to do this would be an act of not loving myself and I have come to learn that learning to love ourselves is one of the most important things we need to do in our life. The Tarot has been a chief factor in this process and both I and my life are better for it.

RESOURCES

The organisations listed below are primarily based in or serving the UK, since I am in the UK. Please look for their equivalent in your own country, or make an initial contact with those here to get more information.

There are of course a great many Charities these days, each with their own particular areas and approach. Those listed are suggestions only and I encourage you to find the one that suits you best.

Reaching out for help is not always easy but it is a real strength to do so, regardless of what your particular need is, or the level of help you feel you might need.

GRIEF

THE GOOD GRIEF TRUST - 'Help and Hope in one place'
https://www.thegoodgrieftrust.org/

THE GOOD GRIEF PROJECT - Understanding Grief as a creative and active process
https://thegoodgriefproject.co.uk/

CRUSE - Bereavement Support
https://www.cruse.org.uk/

MARIE CURIE - Care and Support through terminal illness
https://www.mariecurie.org.uk
https://www.mariecurie.org.uk/help/support/support-directory/bereavement-and-funerals

CHILD BEREAVEMENT UK - Rebuilding Lives Together
https://www.childbereavementuk.org/

AT A LOSS - Helping bereaved people find support
https://www.ataloss.org/

THE LOSS FOUNDATION – Bereavement support for loss to cancer
https://thelossfoundation.org/

WHAT'S YOUR GRIEF – Grief support for the rest of us
https://whatsyourgrief.com/

SLOW – Surviving the loss of your world
https://slowgroup.co.uk/

SUE RYDER – Palliative, neurological and bereavement support
https://www.sueryder.org/about-us

CANCER

YES TO LIFE – The UK's integrative cancer care charity
https://yestolife.org.uk/about-us/

ROY CASTLE LUNG CANCER FOUNDATION – Leading UK lung cancer charity
https://roycastle.org/

PENNY BROHN UK – Living Well with cancer
https://www.pennybrohn.org.uk/

MACMILLAN CANCER SUPPORT – Cancer Info and Support
https://www.macmillan.org.uk/

MENTAL HEALTH

MIND – Advice and support for mental health problems
https://www.mind.org.uk/

SAMARITANS – For anyone who needs someone
https://www.samaritans.org/

NATIONAL HEALTH SERVICE

NHS CHARITIES – helping the NHS go further
https://nhscharitiestogether.co.uk/

STEVE HOUNSOME

www.tarottherapy.co.uk

TAROT THERAPY COURSES

Steve is based in Poole, Dorset, UK and teaches regular Courses and Workshops on the Tarot, by distance-learning and worldwide via Zoom. His focus is on the therapeutic and developmental use of the Tarot, rather than 'fortune-telling'.

There are three levels of Tarot Therapy Courses available -

INTRODUCTION – For those with little or no knowledge or experience of the Tarot, to learn the basics

CERTIFICATE – For those wishing to develop their skills with the Tarot, so they can use it for themselves and others, to a professional level

DIPLOMA – For those with existing knowledge and use of the Tarot, to further develop both themselves and their uses of the Tarot

TRANSFORMATION THROUGH TAROT / THE TAROT CHAKRA JOURNEY

Steve created these two Courses with Philip Carr-Gomm, creator of the Druidcraft Tarot, former Chosen Chief of the Order of Bards, Ovates and Druids, psychologist and author of many books in this field.

These Courses are taken online, with interaction with other students and the creators if you wish.

For more info. - https://artoflivingwell.org.uk/courses

THE SEEKERS QUEST – An in-depth, personal journey through the Major Arcana.

BOOKS
Steve is the author of several books, all available via Amazon, in both printed and digital format. Titles are –

TAROT THERAPY VOL. 1: THE THEORY AND PRACTICE OF
TAROT THERAPY VOL 2: MAJOR ARCANA: THE SEEKERS
QUEST
TAROT THERAPY VOL. 3: MINOR ARCANA: THE MAP OF THE
QUEST
TAMING THE WOLF: FULL MOON MEDITATION
PRACTICAL MEDITATION
PRACTICAL SPIRITUALITY
HOW TO BE A TELEPHONE PSYCHIC
THE TAROT THERAPY DECK
THE GAMBLE-HOUNSOME TAROT: THE TAROT OF GNOSIS

TAROT DECKS AND CARDS

THE GAMBLE-HOUNSOME TAROT: THE TAROT OF GNOSIS – Illustrated by visionary artist Patrick Gamble. Card and book set.

TAROT THERAPY CARDS – A unique Tarot Deck showing the energies of the cards in the natural world. Cards and Book available

CHAKRA AFFIRMATION CARDS – Seven Affirmations for each of the seven Chakras

TAROT THERAPY CONSULTATIONS

Steve gives private one-to-one Consultations, in person in Dorset, UK and worldwide via Zoom.

MEDITATIONS

Steve has available a range of highly-acclaimed, spoken-word meditation and development exercises. These can all be downloaded from the website.

MAILING LIST

To receive a free monthly newsletter from Steve, with all the latest products and teaching available, and exclusive content/special offers, send your email address to:

steve@tarottherapy.co.uk

All details held are completely confidential, are never given out and will be removed on request.

SOCIAL MEDIA

Facebook: TarottherapyUk

Twitter: @HounsomeSteve

Linked In: steve-hounsome

You Tube: Steve Hounsome

Pinterest: Tarot Therapy Ltd

www.tarottherapy.co.uk

www.ingramcontent.com/pod-product-compliance
Lightning Source LLC
Chambersburg PA
CBHW071319090426
42738CB00012B/2736